Career Development:

DESIGNING OUR CAREER MACHINES

David V. Tiedeman
Professor of Education
Northern Illinois University
DeKalb, Illinois

Published simultaneously by:

Character
Research
Press

CARROLL
PRESS

© David V. Tiedeman 1979

Library of Congress Cataloging in Publication Data

Tiedeman, David V.
 Career Development: Designing Our Career Machines

 Bibliography: p. i-xvi, 1-240.
 Includes index.
 1. Vocational guidance—Data processing.
 2. Information storage and retrieval systems—

 Vocational guidance.   I. Title.
 HF5381.T565 1979b   331.7'02'02854

Character Research Press   Carroll Press

ISBN 0-915744-18-X (hardcover)   ISBN 0-910328-27-1 (hardcover)
ISBN 0-915744-11-2 (paperback)   ISBN 0-910328-27-2 (paperback)

Library of Congress Catalog Card No. L.C. 79-14183

Cover Design
by
Robert Olbrycht

(Cover illustration on Carroll Press edition by artist Gordon Brooks.)

Published simultaneously by:

Character Research Press   Carroll Press
 207 State Street   43 Squantum Street
Schenectady, New York 12305   Cranston, Rhode Island 92920

CONTENTS

PREFACE

This is the sixth book on topics in career development, which I have participated in writing. Chronologically, predecessors of **Career Development: Designing Our Career Machine** appeared as follows:

(1963)   Career Development: Choice and Adjustment (with Robert P. O'Hara. New York: College Entrance Examination Board)

(1967)   **Multivariate Statistics for Personnel Classification** (with Phillip J. Rulon, Maurice M. Tatsuoka, and Charles R. Langmuir. New York: John Wiley)

(1976)   **Key Resources in Career Education: An Annotated Guide** (with Marilyn Schreiber and Tyrus R. Wessell. Washington, D.C.: National Institute of Education)

(1977)   **Career Development: Exploration and Commitment** (with Gordon A. Dudley. Muncie, Indiana: Accelerated Development)

(1977)   **Career Development: Designing Self** (with John H. Peatling. Muncie, Indiana: Accelerated Development)

Each of these books stands free on its topic; no one of them is prerequisite to another. However, the publication chronology of the books is not entirely consistent with my own apprehension of decision as generating function in career development and its education. In my epistemological development, the books were created in the following order:

Multivariate Statistics for Personnel Classification (1967)

Career Development: Choice and Adjustment (1963)

Career Development: Exploration and Commitment (1977)

Career Development: Designing Our Career Machines (this book)

Career Development: Designing Self (1977)

Key Resources in Career Education: An Annotated Guide (1977)

Readers interested in the structuring of decisional development into a person's comprehension of career development which I have done might be interested in reading my six books in the above order rather than in their order of publication. **Multivariate Statistics for Personnel Classification** contrasts the classification and selection of personnel and derives a system of multivariate statistics consistent with the logic of classification, not one adapted from the logic of just personnel selection. In this process, the book describes the concept of the multivariate discriminant function using geometric and algebraic representation in parallel when possible so that the one, two, and three variate cases of personnel classification are pictured and the algebraic equivalent is substituted at the fourth variate and beyond when geometric representation becomes visually incomprehensible. Multivariate statistics and their discriminant functions are used in the Career Machine designed in this book.

A great deal of my work on career development during the 1940's and 1950's was devoted to the study of vocational psychology as John Crites (1969) defines it in today's lexicon of career psychology. At that time, I was interested in how persons differed according to the kinds of educations and occupations which they elected to pursue. But in the late 1950's and early 1960's, my work as Professor of Education with responsibility for the Program in Guidance at the Harvard Graduate School of Education brought me in touch with persons who had processes rather than categories of choice predominantly in mind. I was, therefore, drawn, with the aid of Professor Donald E. Super at Teachers College, Columbia University, who has served as unofficial mentor in my study of career development for many years, into the study of both self conceptions and the self concept in career development. My first effort to integrate my thought on personal responsibility in career development was published in 1963 as **Career Development: Choice and Adjustment**. Professor Robert P. O'Hara of Boston College was my colleague in clarifying thought on the processes of choice and decision in career development as those processes were known to another studying them behaviorally. O'Hara and I participated during the germinal years of that book in an informal seminar with Professors Jean Jordaan and Donald Super of Teachers College, Columbia University, and Professors Henry Borow and Ted Volsky of the University of Minnesota. The College Entrance Examination Board provided subvention for the informal seminar and published O'Hara's and my book at the same time as they published **Career Development: Self Concept Theory** by Super and Jordaan with the assistance of Starishevsky and Matlin. Although I can in no way take credit for Super's and Jordaan's work, thorough students of my career development thought might well read **Career Development: Self Concept Theory** coterminally with their reading of **Career Development: Choice and Adjustment**. O'Hara and I proceeded in 1963 on the assumption that career development theory was more encompassing than the functions and processes I articulated. Therefore, I personally related my work to that of Super and Jordaan as the centering of the person into his or her self concept during conscious derivation of career development. In this regard, I borrowed the self concept as focus in career development and elaborated the processes of constructing self conceptions and a self concept through decision in career. My work with O'Hara figures predominantly in the Career Machine designed in this book.

In 1978, I am uncertain whether my work is now better organized under Super's work or his under mine. I incline to the latter view because I have unwaveringly gone to the individual mind as object in career development while Donald Super concentrates upon the behavioral manifestations of vocational development as those manifestations can be known at least to another and frequently only to another. In addition, I have taken the individual in action as my phenomenon of interest in career, not just the individual in the action of work. In this regard, I presently give the word "career" meaning encompassing comprehension of all activity not just vocational activity. This definition organizes **Key Resources in Career Education: An Annotated Guide.** Career education is, of course, today's response to social need for operation of the Career Machine designed in this book.

But I have seemingly leapt a stream without showing my readers the stepping stones I really used in crossing from the bank of vocation to the bank of career. My first stepping stone was the Information System for Vocational Decisions which is the Career Machine whose design, but not reality, several colleagues and I reveal in this book. As of 1966, I undertook an exciting three-year opportunity to design, with a number of colleagues at the Harvard Graduate School of Education, the New England Education Data Systems, the Newton (Massachusetts) School Department and elsewhere, a computer system into which a person might inquire about vocational matters and, in inquiry, join the System for reason not alone of resolving an immediate inquiry but also for further mastery of the individual's inquiry processes themselves. In order to enable such an effect, my ISVD colleagues and I had to design the computer system so that the inquirer collaborates with it to advance its proceduralization with understanding of (a) what was added to the original less partially proceduralized system, (b) how, and (c) why. In doing so, the experience of designing becomes the prime object for the inquirers. When the experience of designing becomes the prime object of inquirers, our design of the system paradoxically becomes the inquirers' design of a sub-system, and the inquirers' comprehension of their design processes enables the inquirers' self direction in career. This use of something tangible to comprehend intangibilities is the basic "I" power process of which Anna Miller-Tiedeman and I will write in a seventh book in my career development series, **Career Development: "I" Power.**

I had to attack two large concepts simultaneously in the design of the Information System for Vocational Decisions. One major problem was the processes of exploration and commitment themselves. Professor Gordon Dudley, who is now at the University of Oregon, and I originally worked out the manuscript on those processes while we worked together in designing the Information System for Vocational Decisions with others. Because of Dudley's tenacity, **Career Development: Exploration and Commitment** saw the light of day before **Career Development: Designing Our Career Machines,** which is really an account of the other major problem in the construction of the Information System for Vocational Decisions, the problem of creating the technically prosthetic mind device which was to have been the operating ISVD.

Personal events in my life, caused me to sideline the technical exposition of the ISVD design until now. In the meantime Dr. John Peatling of the Union College Character Research Project and I published **Career Development: Designing Self.** That book actually builds upon the philosophy and technology of the ISVD reported here to expand the ISVD design into a hypothetical Information System for Life Decisions. In the course of doing that, we presented a group theory of self constructionist personality reconstructionism. The group theory would have been the central epistemological theme I continually sought for ISVD and could not then grasp.

The original material of this book was prepared for annual reports, and in presenting it to my readers largely in its original form my intention is to share with them the creative experience my colleagues and I had in attempting the construction of a Career Machine. As the ISVD contract drew to a close and closed, I realized that the concept of ISVD does not depend upon the existence of an actual Career Machine. All that is needed is active design of a figurative Career Machine by each person, such a figurative Machine being developed sufficiently clearly by each person to carry that person through the uncertainties of mind involved in exploration and commitment to career relevant tasks undertaken with understanding of intentions and operations. That realization gave rise to this book, and as you the reader progress through the book, you will see a shift in our thinking from the Machine as a physical creation to the Machine as a concept. I share this process with you in the conviction that I can help others learn to design their own Career Machine, with which they can further develop their careers, by taking them through the excercise of designing a Machine such as that which my colleagues and I undertook from 1966 to 1969.

I trust that by sharing our experience of creating as we created we can give you a deeper understanding of our process and product than if we had shared only the product. I ask that you bear in mind that ISVD never finally existed as any complete physical being, although the ISVD staff were able to bring into being at least one operating example of every needed part of ISVD. Furthermore, the old incomplete ISVD would today be obsolete just because its operating data files were constructed in the late 1960's, not the late 1970's. Therefore, read this book for the idea of the Career Machine, in order to learn how to build for yourself a relationship with career resources in your environment which will give you additional personal information about your decisions and processes of deciding as you do so. The philosophical, procedural, and technical problems recounted in this volume are indicative of the ones you will have to resolve in the design of your Career Machine. The ISVD solutions to some of them may also help you see solutions which you too will conceive of value. Finally, if you read this volume with sufficient comprehension, upon reflection you will also find that you have had a lesson in how to design. When you cannot fully comprehend something at the start, a good strategy is just to begin, fully knowing that you will have to revise before finishing. A Career Machine is so complicated to design that you have to use that strategy, just as we had to use it. As you use that strategy, you build points of comprehension into the regions of the general problem most relevant to those needs which are more imminent and more clearly understood at that moment. As you proceed, superordinate conceptions will arise allowing you to put then subordinate conceptions into relations with them in the bigger mosaic you can then apprehend. And lo, you will have started a pattern, a design. You will begin to see a whole you were in but could not formerly apprehend, to say nothing of comprehending. If you complete the process enough times, with consciousness expansion in many cases, you will find that you know how to design and have enlarged your confidence in designing for yourself. When you have enough confidence in knowing how to design to live the life of a designer, you have reached a high level of career development. That is what we authors hope this book will help you achieve, the career of life designer.

The design and construction of the prototypic Information System for Vocational Decisions was not an individual effort. Persons who participated in both the design and construction of the System and this book are identified in Appendix A in their noted roles. The project also arose within a context of work I have done with different people. Relevant contextual work and the complete list of ISVD reports are identified in Appendix B.

When you design something, you cooperate with the resources you are then fashioning into different conditions. If you fail to cooperate with your resources, you ordinarily find that your resources fashion you as much if not more than you fashion them, because resources are never passive during the design process, they are always actively setting down conditions which your design must accommodate. In order to leave you in an active state in the design of the Career Machine which was the Information System for Vocational Decision, I have deliberately left the language of this book in the present tense as if ISVD were being designed by the reader and me during the reading rather than having been designed beforehand as it now really was. If I thereby, succeed in bringing the ISVD Career Machine to life in you because of this book, we will both realize that the Career Machine is in us, not in the ISVD. The ISVD was designed with that ethic dominating its construction and this book must remain consistent with it for your education to occur.

DeKalb, Illinois   David V. Tiedeman
January 1978

About the Author

Dr. David V. Tiedeman is Professor of Education at Northern Illinois University, DeKalb, Illinois, and former Director of ERIC Clearing House in Career Education. Throughout his professional life he has contributed to the area of career development.

In 1940 at Harvard University, Tiedeman was involved in translating psychology and psychometrics in the field of education into the practice of guidance and counseling. After earning the Doctor of Education degree, he joined Harvard's faculty as an Instructor in Education in 1949, and became Professor of Education in 1959, a position he held until 1971. Dr. Tiedeman is a member of numerous professional organizations and has held many offices, having been president of American Personnel and Guidance Association.

Dr. Tiedeman resorted once again to the tentativeness in his commitment to guidance in 1971, leaving Harvard to direct Project TALENT at the American Institute for Research, Palo Alto. In 1973 he returned to the university environment to extend his major interest in career development.

Dr. Tiedeman has spent many years researching career development. An early publication was co-authored with Robert P. O'Hara, **Career Development: Choice and Adjustment.** In this volume Tiedeman outlined a theory of personal decision making in career development. His recent works consist of two volumes. The first, **Career Development: Exploration and Commitment,** co-authored with Gordon A. Dudley, provides readers with a comprehensive survey and analysis of many studies and provides readers a primary source document for theory and research in the growing field of career development. The second in the series, **Career Development: Designing Self,** co-authored with John H. Peatling, is about knowing self and personality construction theory and offers a design for three successively more complex interactive Information Systems for Vocational Decisions, Educational Decisions and Self Decisions.

Section I

SETTING AND INTENTIONS

SETTING

Career Theory Swings from an Occupational to a Career Psychology[1]

Ginzberg, Ginsburg, Axelrad, and Herma electrified the field of vocational psychology in 1951 with their book, Occupational Choice: An Approach to General Theory. In the first place, Ginzberg and associates focused attention in the field away from occupational success and toward occupational choice. In the second place, they introduced time into the study of vocational psychology. Finally, they formulated initial propositions about developmental stages and periods associated with occupational choice from childhood to young adulthood. The occupational choice is supposed to advance from the condition of fantasy into the conditions of reality and preliminary trial in those ages.

The book by Ginzberg and his associates challenged Professor Donald E. Super, Teachers College, Columbia, to organize a new field of career psychology. Super did so in two major steps. Super's first major step was to propose a theory of vocational development (1953). The ten propositions in Super's theory centered occupational choice in the self concept and made the development of the vocational self concept

[1]Adapted from "Career Education: A Guidance Idea Reaches Its Term," by David V. Tiedeman as published by *Quest*, 1974, 8(3) 1-4.

DESIGNING OUR CAREER MACHINES   1

within the multipotentiality of each individual the primary subject of vocational development.

Super's second major step was publication of **The Psychology of Careers** (1957). This now classic book incorporated his theory of vocational development into a life development framework. In one stroke Super thereby changed the study of vocational psychology from the study of singular vocational events into the interactive and multitudinous vocational events which happen from birth to death. He proposed that vocational development can be expected to progress through stages of growth, transition, trial, maintenance, and decline. Career patterns take shape and find expression or give frustration within such a developmental framework.

Implementing the New Career Psychology

Career Guidance: A First Step

The 1950's saw the noted swing from an occupational to a career psychology. The 1960's saw new social forces coalesce with the new career development theory to imprint upon the practice of guidance. Professionally the forces at play in guidance were ones which focused upon the necessity of doing individual counseling long enough and well. The theoretical underpinnings of those forces originated in psychotherapy and had marked influence on the changing practice. The fact that Ginzberg (1971) correctly hypothesizes a conflict rather than a confluence between counseling and career is one of the shames in the guidance field. Actually, the work of Bordin, Nachmann and Segal (1963), Holland (1959), Roe (1956), Super (1957), and Tiedeman and O'Hara (1963) all emphasize the interplay of psychology and work. Intensive and extensive interviewing and counseling are needed to bring these understandings to the forefront of the ones counselors help. But therapy and career must be united *in the person.*

Former U.S. Commissioner of Education, Sidney P. Marland Jr. brought developments in career psychology to a practical head in 1971 just after being named to his Commissionership. Dr. Marland entered his new office determined to improve education. He singled out career education as a major means to improve education. Upon his appointment as U.S. Commissioner of Education, Dr. Marland quickly announced his intentions for the field of career education at the 1971 Convention of the Association of Secondary School Principals meeting in Convention at Houston, Texas. At this Convention Dr. Marland proposed that " . . . life and how to live it is the primary vocation of all of us. And the ultimate test of our educational process, on any level, is how close it comes to preparing our people to be alive and active with their hearts, and their minds, and for many, their hands as well." (p. 9) With this goal, Marland then took off from Dr. Grant Venn's conclusion in his **Man, Education, and Manpower,** (1970), namely, "If we want an educational system designed to serve each individual and to develop his creative potential in a self-directing way, then we have work to do and attitudes to change." (p. 4) According to Dr. Marland, " . . . All our efforts as educators must be bent on preparing students either to become properly, usefully employed immediately upon graduation from high school or to go on to further formal education." (p. 5) This is the goal for the work we must do and the attitudes we must change.

The Challenge of the Developmental Idea at Its Term:
The Third Step

As indicated, career education is not a new idea; it is an idea whose investigative roots go back to the years of World War II. What is new about career education is that the power and resolve of the U.S. Office of Education is currently being put behind the conception. Will counselors seize this idea in its term and see that the child has an orderly and considerable growth or will they sit on the sidelines as others work the current public will? This is the challenge which Dr. Marland left counselors near the close of his service as Assistant Secretary of Health, Education, and Welfare.

Former Assistant Secretary Marland issued this challenge to the members of the American Personnel and Guidance Association meeting in Convention in San Diego, California, February 9, 1973. Dr. Marland (1973) challenged counselors this way: "As counselors, you are really at the heart of what might be the most significant reform movement in education since universal education became our watchword. I ask that you think hard about assuming that central role of orchestrating the many parts of education that must flow together if career education is to become a reality." (p. 4)

INTENTIONS

Initiation

The United States Office of Education seems to have had Marland's career education idea in mind before he arrived on the scene as its Commissioner. That Office and the President and Fellows, Harvard College, entered into agreement as of June 1, 1966 to support and construct the prototype of a computer-based Information System for Vocational Decisions (ISVD). The prototype was to be delivered on or before July 1, 1969, thirty-seven months from the date of initiation.

Part of the purpose of this book is to describe the Information System for Vocational Decisions which grew from that contract. The ISVD offers foundation for the career development education which Marland advocated upon assumption of his Commissionership. As you read this book, I trust you grow in appreciation of a science which can undergird career development without limitation of personal responsibility. As my colleagues and I began the design of the Career Machine which became ISVD, we found that the discipline of the computer medium in which we worked immediately required us to integrate the various pieces of vocational psychology into a career psychology. Chapter 1 represents my first creation of such an integration.

Chapter 1 is followed by chapters in three other sections in which additional specification of missing parts of an operational theory of career development had to be supplied. Section II first summarizes the ISVD design in form necessary to focus upon the place of language in the development of the career within the self. The Section then presents two examples of the high degree to which the theory of counseling has to be specified in order to have it play within a Career Machine creating awareness of career development, rather than the limitation of career growth. In this regard, Chapters 3 and 4 serve as foundation to CLIENT 1 which Hummel, Lichtenberg, and Shaffer (1975) devised and operate at the University of Minnesota. CLIENT 1 is a standard client programmed to respond to counseling students according to a theory of counseling as these students try to operate upon that theory. Hummel, Lichtenberg, and Shaffer found that they had to plow deeply into the top soil of our alleged counseling theory in order to program some of the effects which exist in real life situations but are hard to simulate when you proceduralize what seems to happen naturally. The ISVD staff faced similar problems which are described in greater detail in Chapters 3 and 4. Programming a Counseling or Career Machine requires very careful attention to the theory of both.

Section III makes the leap which became the central ISVD assumption, namely that to grow in control of career, individuals have to grow in the design (or further proceduralization) of their personal career machines. This theme is elaborated in Section III so that it has application in the personal designs of a Counseling Machine, a Career Machine, and an Admissions Machine.

Finally, Section IV, takes the additional step of specifying a theory of guidance in society within the discipline of machine design used throughout this book as the needed specific means of articulating what we know and how we know. In that Section, the machine design concept is first extended from that of the three Machines designed in Section III to the design of an Education Machine. Finally, that concept is extended to the design of a Person Machine.

The association of computers in the achievement of the purposes of guidance and counseling does not rest easy on professionals in these fields. But I consider computers essential to the attainment of the purposes of guidance and counseling. Furthermore, I believe that the attainment of some of the purposes of guidance and counseling with the provision of a computer-involved system which prosthetic to the minds of those interacting with the system, frees counselors and other educators to seek higher order outcomes for their activities than is now common.

Designing the Information System for Vocational Decisions proved to be my personal route to these understandings. This book invites you to design an Information System for Vocational Decision of your own so that we may together markedly accelerate our understanding of the individual processes involved in the individuation with cooperation.

Objective

The major objective of the ISVD was to improve vocational decision-making through the use of a computer-based training system. The program was to be so designed that students could relate knowledge about themselves to data about education, training, and work and thereby create a body of information on which they could base their career decisions. The entire program linked person, computer, and teacher or counselor in such a way that the student could conduct a dialogue with the computer, while the counselor assisted in interpreting and evaluating the results of the dialogue.

CAREER DEVELOPMENT

PROBLEM AS STIPULATED IN PROJECT PROPOSAL

The following statement is quoted in full from the original proposal entitled, "An Information System for Vocational Decisions," submitted by D. V. Tiedeman, E. Landy, W. J. Fletcher, A. B. Ellis, R. G. Davis, and E. G. Boyer, Principal Investigators to the U.S. Commissioner of Education under the provisions of Section 4(c) of the Vocational Education Act of 1963.

"... participation in an occupation involves more than training in the specific skills required. Before, during, and even after vocational training the process of *decision-making* must also be involved. Central in decisions about occupations, jobs, or courses of study are facts/data* about one's self and about work. Facts illumine and frequently create decisions particularly when facts are given the status of data by inquirers. But decisions also create facts. This account of the project therefore provides opportunity to study the interaction of facts and decision, and their subsequent creation of information.

"The proposed ISVD will deliberately play upon a potentially useful distinction between *data* (facts) and *information* (interpreted facts). The task of the information system is to enable the individual to transform data into information. This is to be done by teaching students to interpret the data in the light of their knowledge, experience, and intention, so that their organization and use of the data represents their own personal relationship to them in the process of decision-making. We presume that only when data are used in this way can they be described as information where the individual is concerned. The information so generated can then, in turn, serve as data in the making of future decisions.

*Occupational facts/data come in two conditions, fixed and modifiable. We therefore elect to adopt the cumbersome term, "facts/data," to indicate this fact throughout the book. Occupational facts are directly recoverable without modification except for storage and later retrieval. On the other hand, occupational data consist of facts which must be additionally processed by the numeric and/or linguistic routines of a modifying system. Either unmodified facts or previously modified data need to be further mediated if they are to be turned into information. This is why we refer conjointly to facts/data whenever our connotation is associated with information.

"Given that the quality of decisions is directly related to the kind, quality, and comprehensiveness of the *information* (i.e., data in relation to personal intention) considered by the individual during the process of decision-making, then a fundamental task of guidance is to identify, evaluate, and classify needed information *and to make it readily available to counselors and students in useable forms and at needed times and places.* A second task is to learn how past decisions can be used to create information of value to the students who have made those decisions. We speak first of the provision and display of data, and its transformation into information. When we consider the teaching of decision-making, we will discuss the creation of further information by the analysis of past decisions.

"Guidance workers have had difficulty in providing and effectively displaying data. This is so because the amount of these data is directly related to the unparalleled rate of change in the technological world, which in turn is rapidly producing basic changes in our society. If we are to prepare students with skills, and attitudes and understanding for a changed and continuously changing future, we must know something of the nature of the changes involved. We must also encourage students to think of vocational planning as a *lifetime* process, not a one-time decision. 'The counselor must think *future* and not experience or he will be of diminishing value to the student of the sixties and seventies' (Wrenn, 1962, p. 20).

"Not only have counselors found it difficult to provide and display data, but the relatively infrequent contact between student and counselor has made the student's interpretation of data largely a hit-or-miss affair. Most students in secondary schools see a counselor three or four times a year at most. Furthermore, the nature of these contacts is frequently governed by a concern for the immediate next decision to be made ("What courses shall I take next term?") and the immediate interest of the student ("I'm interested in science."). The amount and quality of facts available to the counselor at the time of an interview is limited by his own knowledge and his school's resources. And the counselor's usual function is to provide facts for the student at the same time (and frequently without distinction) that he is attempting to get the student to use them.

"What is needed is a system which will provide for the student direct access to all relevant facts without requiring the *direct* mediation of a counselor. This would bring about a change in the counselor's role. Instead of being *both* source and interpreter of facts, he would have the primary responsibility of interpreting the student's *use* of the facts as he transforms them into information. This would require attention to the role of unconscious motivation, and the effort to help the student transform his tacit understandings into explicit ones. Also included in his role would be training the student in the use of the data system, supervising him in its use, and evaluating the student's decision-making process. Ultimately, it should be possible for the student to use the data system in a relatively independent manner for both exploration and decision-making, with recourse to the counselor only when assistance or interpretation is needed.

"Another important factor in the decision-making process is the student's 'sense of agency,' that is his awareness, that he is an active agent in determining the course of his own career (Field 1964). We feel that many persons, especially those in economically depressed areas who have been socially and culturally deprived, may lack this 'sense of agency' because of a lack of accurate information about themselves and their real ability* to act on their environment.

"This proposal is in part an outgrowth of a study conducted during 1964-65 by John B. Carroll and Allan B. Ellis under contract with the U.S. Office of Education (Contract No. OE-5-10-097) (Carroll and Ellis, 1965). The study was undertaken to determine the nature of a possible data bank and the role such a bank should play in the development of a systematic education program for the New England region. A significant conclusion reached by the investigators was that an educational data bank should not be a static storehouse. To be of real value to the process of education, a data bank must be dynamic enough to become a functional part of the education process.

"This conclusion was of special interest to the New England Education Data Systems (NEEDS), which was established in 1963 by the New England School Development Council and which is affiliated with the Harvard Graduate School of Education as well as the 57 other organizations. NEEDS is an effort to bring the technology of data processing to bear on the administrative, curricular and guidance problems of the schools of New

England. A long-term objective of NEEDS is to establish a regional information center for its member school systems so that as NEEDS grows, a large body of data will be available to facilitate educational research and development efforts in the region. This proposal is therefore designed to take a major step toward the development of such a comprehensive regional information center in the area of vocational education."

Chapter 1

THE INFORMATION SYSTEM
FOR VOCATIONAL DECISIONS (ISVD)[1]

THESIS AND ETHIC

The intent of the Information System for Vocational Decisions was to place an inquirer in potentially repeated interaction with a computer-centered environment programmed for individual inquiry, not just for prompt reinforcing of stimulus-response continguity. The context for the inquiries would be education, occupation, military service, and personal and family living. The inquirer may elect at will among contexts. The System could be constructed so as to expect the inquirer to learn how to harmonize personal goals and their consequences by means of repeated inquiries in these four important realms of personal activity.

Inquiry
Not
Reinforcement

As noted, the primary goal of the ISVD was to be inquiry, not reinforcement. Because our System was intended to put inquirers in *direct* relation with their evolving history and intentions to the extent that such can be motivated and represented through the numbers, letters, and processing available in computer reckoning, should it become possible to avoid one of the fears which the public has of using computers in

---

[1]This chapter was written by David V. Tiedeman.

guidance, namely the fear that computers will determine lives by making decisions *for*, not *with*, persons. Our System was planned to let any inquirer experience practically the same joy and frustration which computer devotees daily do, namely the realization that the answer is in them, not in the machine. Despite any inquirer's occassional regret upon such realizations, they know that they still persevere. Therefore, the assumption of the ISVD was that *any* person can and will persevere through inquiry. A further assumption of the ISVD was that repeatedly experienced failure to find full solutions to questions can be fashioned into mature capacity for proceeding on inadequate bases in adult life, as inquirers are brought to realize the care we used in fashioning a System which can take them down the path of, *but never completely into*, awareness of the operation of their motivational systems.

Because of the above conviction, we planned to assemble a System different from others imagined in computer-aided instruction or in educational data processing. The ISVD subsumed both of these conceptions as *intermediate* in the condition of education for responsible career decisions. However, our own primary professional task was the construction of a meta-system which could permit analysis and response direction in terms of the majority of the variables of this expected responsibility.

Psychologists ordinarily study vocational development as it exists, thereby avoiding consideration of what it might be. The ISVD was planned to do the contrary, namely, focus on vocational development as it might well be. In doing so, our attempt was both to take advantage of vocational psychologists' studies of what vocational development now is and to cultivate the career concept in which we believe.

**Dimensions of
Vocational
Development**

The specific dimensions of vocational development which

we attempted to augment are:

1. the placing of occupation into vocational development as but a single instance of vocational expression which can be repeated many times during a life;

2. the offering of responsibility to students and workers for many choices in relation to education, work, leisure, and marriage;

3. the extension of opportunity for occupational choice and preparation down into the elementary grades and out into work until retirement; and

4. the provision of an explicit educational context within which students and workers can be made aware of the value of fantasy, imagination, and preconscious experience for maintaining some continuity in their personality organization and careers, while permitting discontinuity in educational and occupational opportunities to be incorporated into their concepts of personality and career.

The faith of the System was to be that intuition disciplined by reason offers the chief "guiding" mechanism for us in our democracy and for humans in their vocationalized lives.

THE CAREER AND ITS CHOICES IN THE COURSE OF CAREER DEVELOPMENT

The context of vocational decision-making offers excellent opportunity for realizing our intention when the computer is given centrality, but necessary incompleteness, in the interacting system in which career development emerges. We define career as personally-given direction in developing vocational activity. We bind a career by expecting that the exercise of personal intention brings with it accountability for self-directed activity. Therefore, we expect that career development requires the emergence of self-initiated activity for which persons permit themselves to be held to account. When persons do so, we can give power to the process of social control by encouraging the independence of freedom and the interdependence of social consciousness.

Contexts for
Career Decisions

Forming a career involves a *set* of decisions which are made throughout life. These decisions are made in the context of education, vocation, military service, and family. The object, plan, and progress of decisions in each of these areas have their own characteristics which we comment upon in the next section. The socially-determined choice contexts in which progress in career takes place are as follows:

Education

There are six primary choice contexts in which educational histories are forged. Each of these contexts also has a subsidiary context which we note. The primary contexts with their subsidiary contexts are:

Choice of secondary school curriculum. The subsidiary choices relate to the kind and level of curriculum and to the specification of skill area within each kind and level.

Choice of post-secondary education. Subsidiary choices in a post-secondary education election include the kind and level of opportunity. As final choice of post-secondary education nears, a specific school and/or college must be differentiated from a more general context. This specific differentiation involves choice as a part of a post-secondary education placement function.

Choice of a collegiate major. The choice of college major involves choices of kinds of majors and a later differentiation of potential emphasis in terms of analysis, synthesis, and/or reduction to practice in the elected major.

Choice of a graduate school. The graduate school choice is similar in context to the choice of a college (see above). *Choice of graduate specialization.* Specialization in graduate school continues the specification of prior college majors in the several areas of knowledge (see above). However, at this time the emphases on analysis, synthesis, and reduction to practice must become clear cut and must be pursued avidly. At the master's level there is likely to be an emphasis on the technology of a subject; at the doctor's level an emphasis on professional activity.

Choices related to the further refining of occupational location by both job and position emphases within general vocational activity. These job and position choices find interrelation with endeavors organized as continuing education.

Vocation

There are three primary choice contexts associated with vocational development itself. Each primary context also has its subsidiary contexts. The primary and subsidiary contexts are:

Entry job. This choice involves a first choice of kind and level of occupation. As entry into work nears, the choice must be sufficiently differentiated so that work is initiated in a specific job. This differentiation involves occupational choice with the placement function.

Job Progress. Choices bringing about job progress initiate the emergence of a career. If individuals attempt to conceive their job movements in a personal historical context in which they also conceive their own vocational activity as progression, they initiate career considerations into their vocational development.

Position and career choices. As individuals develop a sense of progress in their occupational activities, they begin to focus upon jobs, not occupations; then upon positions, not jobs; and finally upon career, not work. These kinds of choices become salient around midlife if they become salient at all.

Military Service[2]

There are three primary kinds of choices associated with the military service aspect of vocational behavior. These primary contexts are:

Kind of Service. The person must differentiate between army, navy, marines, coast guard, and air force.

Level of service. A prime issue at the beginning of military service is the distinction between *enlisted* and *officer* status. Some persons start right off to prepare for officer status. However, in either status, promotion also becomes an issue in its proper time as determined by the regulations of a service.

Specialization. Within enlisted ranks in particular, choice of specialization becomes important. In the officer's ranks, specialization is likely to be present but not stressed to that degree in which it is stressed in enlisted ranks.

Personal and Family Living

There are two primary contexts for choice in the family area. They are:

Marriage. There must be a decision about marriage or not. If marriage is elected, a further decision relates to when in life it should occur and/or re-occur. As noted, the marriage context also involves a choice about continuation in marriage with divorce being the legal means for separation, termination, and potential reinvolvement.

[2] Males in the United States are not subject to draft in 1978 as they were in 1966 when this was written. The data file is left as it was planned in 1966 because it received special attention throughout our design of ISVD. However, the military data file could just be a sub-aspect of the vocational data file in a 1978 ISVD.

Family. Style of life in family is also an area in which choice takes place. This area involves choices of size of family, location of household, culture with regard to extended family living, and the balance of time among work, family, and recreation.

THE SYSTEM

General
Framework

The Information System for Vocational Decisions was deliberately named despite the fact that our connotations for its words were not presently entirely a matter of common parlance. The word, "Information," was and is still intended to connote the inquirers' placing of facts/data into their personal context of use. This use of the word emphasized our belief that facts/data require the context of use if they are to be conceived as information.

Students and workers would be enabled to turn educational and occupational facts/data into information through the System by assuming an inquiring attitude. Thus, users would become an explicit part of our connotation of "System." Our connotation reflects our intention to offer each user complete responsibility in the choice of educational and vocational goals. Although it is probably inevitable that the computer will be blamed for "error," we did not intend to let the users of our System enjoy the luxury of that impression without contest. The contest was to be the chief motivational device of the System and constitutes the primary context for professional supervision in the System.

The possibility for user determination of data processing in the System could be provided by a time-shared (or time-sliced as some prefer) computer potential. User-computer interaction becomes possible in the time-shared mode of modern large-scale computers. In that time-shared mode, the user (1) can make direct input into the computer under guidance from its predetermined routines, (2) can direct the processing of this input and other stored facts/data, and (3) can determine somewhat the form and content of the output. The speed of modern computers makes it seem as if there were no delay in the user's access to the computer. Actually there is delay, but the trick in establishing the operating computer programs governing the System could be to minimize that delay for the several users who will be in interaction with the computer at the same time. To the extent that delay might become a factor in our System, the System would not service the needs of the users when they were exploring. For exploration, the mood being simulated in the interacting must be that of browsing.

Data Files

The ISVD was planned to have a data file for each of the previously noted four areas of living: occupation, education, military service, and personal and family living. Data in each file would range from general to specific in accord with the anatomy of choice in career development which was sketched above. In addition, data would schematically attempt both to represent the present and to outline the future for a decade or so, such outlining being in small time increments. These specifications obligate the System to deal with overall data on local job markets as well as to incorporate data on specific local job vacancies which will be helpful in making placement suggestions.

The fifth data file in the System was planned to contain inquirer characteristics. This file was to be in two parts. One part dealt with the characteristics of inquirers in general and reported on the relationships of these characteristics to the later choices and successes of those inquirers. This file could be used both to suggest alternatives to users who need wider scope for consideration and to subject aspiration to the test of "reality" when the user is in a condition clarifying a preferred alternative. The other part of the inquirer characteristic data file comprised the private educational and occupational history of the user as portrayed in the context of the user's developing justifications for personal preferences and their pursuit with evolving consequences.

Decision-Making: The Paradigm for Choosing

Reflection upon facts/data of the several areas was to be encouraged with the expectation that the facts/data would be put to personal use. The personal use to which these facts/data could be put was additionally expected to become guided by a paradigm of vocational decision-making (Tiedeman and O'Hara, 1963). This paradigm essentially conceives decision in relation (1) to the passage of time, and (2) to the undertaking of the risk and activity required to achieve what one elects to achieve. This conception permits division of the time interval into a period of anticipation and a period of accommodation. Anticipation occurs before the activities of a socially delineated discontinuity become required; accommodation occurs after such activity is required. Stages of exploration, crystallization, choice, and clarification are distinguished within the period of anticipation. Stages of induction, reformation, and integration become possible within the period of accommodation. Distinctions among these stages would be a central part of a MONITOR computer routine in the ISVD.

Computer Routines

Computer routines and supporting materials were to be fashioned to conform to the expectation that this vocational decision paradigm both exists and can become explicit and useful to someone who practices its use. The paradigm delineates but not completely determines the computer routines which we were to develop to permit access to each of the data files and to provide data upon request. There were to be three *primary* computer routines: REVIEW, EXPLORATION, and CLARIFICATION.

The present operational versatility of the computer does not permit direct simulation of all the periods and stages of the paradigm of decision-making. For this reason, for each choice in career development, the three stages of the period of accommodation were all to be incorporated within the REVIEW access routine. The four stages of the period of anticipation in any kind of decision-making can each be more closely approximated in computer simulation. The System would therefore have an EXPLORATION access routine which would presume the modes of exploration leading to crystallization in the period of anticipation. The System would also have a CLARIFICATION computer routine. The CLARIFICATION computer routine would presume exploration, crystallization, and choice and engage the inquirer in questions of clarifying a previously designated alternative.

The REVIEW computer routine would permit call up and comparison of a prior statement about what had been a then future event both after that expected future event has occurred and after the user has provided an indication of how prior expectations were fulfilled. The procedure would expect a person to experience insight with regard to consistency and inconsistency available during comparison, and to learn from such insight that personal intuition guides personal activity. The intended outcome of REVIEW was that users learn from their history.

The EXPLORATION computer routine would allow the person to rove through a data file as near randomly as possible. The routine would encourage the use of randomness largely at only general levels of materials in order to conserve time but will not forbid specific exploration if, and when, desired. Furthermore, routines could be developed to suggest alternatives on the basis of comparing personal characteristics with established associations between such characteristics of others and their preferred alternatives. The intended outcome from this routine was the emergence of (1) a set of alternatives, and (2) the bases on which the alternatives are preferred. Achievement of the second of these outcomes brings further awareness of the reasoning process which is actually involved in career development.

The CLARIFICATION computer routine would be available after specific alternatives are selected. CLARIFICATION would take inquirers into queries about the depth of their knowledge concerning the then favored alternatives and the understanding of future alternatives which are likely linked with present preferences. The outcome desired from CLARIFICATION would be the dispelling both of some doubt and of some ignorance concerning the next step in the progress of career which the person is evolving. Lessening both doubt and ignorance is likely to increase the inquirer's confidence in meeting the activities required by the next step.

In addition to the three primary computer routines, MONITOR would be available as the only *secondary* computer routine. MONITOR would essentially consist of the evaluations which we were able to concoct to determine the mastery of stages in the paradigm of vocational decision-making. For this reason, MONITOR would have to be able to play back into, as well as over, the computer inputs which the person generates. There would be three essential aspects of MONITOR. The first aspect could be the actual procedure which we concocted and programmed the computer to provide. The second aspect would be the bases on which we caused our judgments to operate among the data put in by each person during interaction with the computer. The third aspect would be the basic computer routines themselves which users would be taught to use if and when they desired to have them. This aspect would make it possible for the user to write individual monitoring bases to some extent and to have these personal monitoring procedures play among personal material just as ours was planned to originally. We hoped through MONITOR to encourage mastery of the concept of feedback and to give practice and supervision in its application.

Materials

The computer routines would incorporate the vocational decision-making paradigm. We did not expect that the computer-directive materials would themselves be sufficient to mature fully the capacity and confidence for use of the decision-making paradigm. We therefore planned to design two other activities into the System in its totality. One of these other activities was to be the simulation of decision-making. Simulation could be available in (1) games, (2) booklets in which the concepts are taught, and (3) decision problems of a vocational nature which must be solved in interaction with the computer.

The second of our other activities which we hoped would further mature the use of the paradigm of vocational decision-making was to be the actual provision of responsibility for work under laboratory and practice conditions. In laboratory and practice, reality can replace imagination if there is intentful supervision of our users as they practice. This supervision should probably be of the same nature as that employed by counselors with inquirers as they are engaged in the simulated activities of vocational decision-making during the inquirer-computer interactions.

Our materials would have to be compatible with computer use and must contribute to education for vocational decision-making. We planned to attempt to make visual and typewritten inputs available to our inquirers under direction from the computer. Oral input must be made with the direct aid of counselors or after their later review of a tape recorder. On line, oral input is not yet reliably available in modern computers.

We planned to attempt to make pictorial and word outputs available to our inquirers as well as auditory outputs. The coordination of our input and output modes with the several modes of the decision-making paradigm will test our imaginations to the limits.

CAREER: THE MATURATION OF PERSONAL RESPONSIBILITY THROUGH VOCATIONAL DEVELOPMENT

We have so far attempted to show that the Information System for Vocational Decisions was planned to expect choice and could cultivate the capacity for and confidence in choosing by giving users almost infinite possibility for the exercise of decision-making among data bases while simultaneously attempting to make the processes of decision-making both explicit and mastered. These are elements in vocational development which had previously neither been unified in this manner nor made available for practice in modes in which complexity is possible but time is not of the essence, at least not the time of persons other than the person engaged in the exercise. The existence of the System would therefore be a first-time physical representation of the "outside" which the person must first learn to bring "inside" and then to act toward knowing that it is there but knowing that one need not be "driven" by it if the individual is the master of it.

In its totality the System could represent "reality" in its data bases, offer processes for working with facts/data through its primary computer routines, and provide practice for integration of a differentiated condition. The System could provide practice under supervision through (1) its secondary computer routines, (2) its simulation of decision-making, and (3) its personal supervision (a) by a counselor of the person in interaction in the computer routine and (b) by a vocational educator as the inquirer assumes real work responsibility in laboratory and practice work situations.

The person who through living comes to master structure and process in this way and comes to a comfortable and integrated accommodation to both, has mastered the architectonics of vocational development. Such a person has both developed and been tutored in the capacity to consider personal development and to engage in the thoughtful activity which puts the individual into development. This is possible through vocational development in which the "myths" of "others" and "authorities" are available in machines but where interactions with their pronouncements are encouraged in ways in which all are eventually disclosed as being only partial and never completely accurate. By offering persons opportunity to come in contact with the best of the known and to learn that the best of the known is still not Truth, it becomes gradually possible for them to realize their own possibilities and responsibilities in representing their desires and aspirations. Through the practice of aspiring in the System, the inquirer first has a "crutch" for the expression and testing of aspiration. It remains for the supervisors of the System to make sure that the "crutch" is later abandoned but that return for data/facts is not denied when they can usefully contribute to later decisions.

We speak of a mature condition in vocational development which is only approximated, never fully attained in all regards with all decisions. However, through patience and practice, persons should be able to achieve more mastery of the processes required for thought in action than is presently the case.

Processes of thought in action mature slowly. This is why we expected the System to span a range from elementary school to retirement.

Processes of thought in action require practice and feedback as well as the exercise of imagination. This is why the System starts in imagination but spans reality through simulation of reality and through supervision of activity in real condition.

Vocational educators recognize in their daily activities the need for reality as test for imagination. This is an important reason why the Information System must embrace vocational education. Since vocational education is a form of education in which reality enters into education, it is a shame to attempt to make vocational education more "general" by sacrificing education for a role under expert supervision while vocational experience is being acquired. Instead, we should attempt to make vocational education more specific to the goal of role incorporation. The vocationalization of preference and activity depends as much, if not more, on education for the understanding of choice and role acquisition as it does on training for occupational skills. Vocational educators would therefore do well first to insure that their colleagues in general education did not forget to train for relevant occupational skills through their "general" curriculum, and second to concentrate their own attention on the socialization processes which are involved in developing understanding in relation to the processes of choosing and role acquisition. Such priorities would (1) place a general goal into the specific interests of vocational educators, (2) make both general and vocational educators accountable for the specifics of vocational education, but (3) still leave vocational educators with an extremely important stake in education for career.

Chapter 2

INFORMATION GENERATION:
FROM FACTS/DATA TO INFORMATION[1]

GENERATING ENGLISH IN THE GUIDING MECHANISM

As has been noted, the basic aim of the ISVD was designed to help inquirers to create a language structure in harmony with their evolving vocational development. In the ISVD, the computer would assist in the processes both of vocational development and of its harmonization with personal career development.

The personal career development which we hoped the ISVD would attempt to cultivate presumes the existence of discontinuities in the person's vocational development. A discontinuity has both external and internal referents. The external referents are those aspects of the societal structure which precipitate discontinuity of personality development by virtue of forcing choice in order not to have a prescribed set of experiences and requirements for all citizens. In the ISVD, these external referents were to be keyed to the educational, occupational, military, and personal and family living decisions which are available in the United States.

The internal referents of discontinuities are those aspects of ego processes which give rise to and/or support the emergence of self awareness in career development. The internal referents emphasize the continuities of personality during

[1] This chapter continues the argument on information generation originally appearing in Project Report Number 12, "The Role of Decision-Making in Information Generation: An Emerging New Potential in Guidance," by David V. Tiedeman.

the meeting of a discontinuity of society. As such they tend to stress the integrative aspects of personality in career development in relation to the differentiating aspects of society in vocational development. These internal referents are thus the potentially harmonizing conditions in the linguistic differentiation of vocational development which the ISVD was to seek to cultivate during career development.

The ISVD would assume that a process is discernible and explicable during any meeting of the externals and internals associated with a societally-generated discontinuity in life. The ISVD would further assume that this process is analyzable by us and eventually by the person experiencing the discontinuity into anticipatory and accommodating phases. The Tiedeman and O'Hara (1963) theory of decision-making on which this assumption is predicated further assumes that the phase of accommodation is both publicly and personally analyzable in terms of the steps of exploration, crystallization, choice and clarification and that the phase of accommodation is also publicly and personally analyzable in terms of the steps of induction, reformation, and integration.

The ISVD was planned to bring the users attention upon the processes of vocational development for reasons of their achieving further harmony in career development. This attention can be sought both in a machine and in a personal context. In the machine context, the persons interacting with the System could be treated as if they are inquirers, persons who are themselves in search of answers for problems which they are generating and who are also willing and able to assume responsibility for the actions predicated upon such inquiries. For this reason, the machine context of the ISVD could consist on the one hand of the primary data files which have been outlined briefly in the prior section.

The inquirer's searches of primary data files would also have to be mediated by the computer in some of its aspects. This mediation was to be designed in the ISVD as if we were teaching a guidance machine to understand English. This stance was necessary in the ISVD in order to keep the subject's interaction as that of inquiry. However, the stance was more importantly necessary because the "game" of the System was to facilitate the incorporation of the English which the guidance machine was able to understand into the English upon which inquirers become ever more aware that they have predicated their vocational and career developments. Thus, through teaching, practice, and interpersonal relations, the ISVD expected the incorporation of the English understanding of the System into linguistic structures of the person. MONITOR was to be a central concept for this incorporation. MONITOR was to be a System control for checking the inquirers' understanding of the linguistic framework of their vocational and career developments. MONITOR would also consist of the rules and processes which went into our creation of that control. Through this means, the ISVD would expect that inquirers would permit themselves to be guided by our control and come to life by the internal operation of their intelligence as they grow in wisdom about their career development. "MONITOR" was to be our way of expressing the stage of the generalization which was to be taken over by each person in their machine interaction. Supervision by counselors and instructors would be our way of further generalizing "MONITOR" in order to complete its internalization and operation in everyday practice by the individual.

The teaching of the guidance machine to understand English and the incorporation of that process because of interaction with an inquirer would give rise to the machine operations which have been previously referred to as those of the secondary data files. Secondary data files must be planned to operate in two ways. One of the ways that secondary data files must operate is subsidiary to primary data files when matters of accuracy in inquiry of those files are in focal attention. The other way in which the secondary data files must operate is superordinate to the primary data files when the teaching and practice of decision-making is in focal attention. It was in this superordinate operation of the primary data files that the hard design puzzles of teaching MONITOR and "MONITOR" to understand English actually rested. This sketch of the ISVD was neither easy to construct nor to understand. However, we trust that we have now created enough both of a review of the prior section and of an overview of terms and later discussion so that we are justified in proceeding with more of the detail of *how* ISVD could actually be structured so that some of its aims might be realized.

INFORMATION FROM FACTS/DATA

The details of the primary and secondary data files noted in the prior section were to be an inherent part only of the ISVD. However, the information processes which are also inherent in the concepts of the primary and subsidiary data files have more general applicability extending to all library data processed with the help of a computer. A particularly significant library project of this nature in the United States is that of the several ERIC Clearinghouses. Each ERIC Clearinghouse is responsible for specific subject(s). Staff members in each Clearinghouse are responsible for assembling and abstracting published literature in their subject and for servicing requests for references in that literature. The subject of guidance and counseling is handled at the University of Michigan under direction of Professor Gary Walz. We particularly refer to Walz' contributions to the theory of information generation as we proceed to consider that theory and the ISVD.

Walz and Rich (1967) have a significant article on ERIC and its potential contribution to the practice of student personnel services. In this article, Walz and Rich first describe the processes of abstracting, indexing, and cross-referencing reduced information as we have somewhat described those processes in the preceding section. They then go on to consider both the predictable outcomes of those processes and their implications for student personnel services as well. These predictions and their implications constitute a potential possible in ERIC but not yet thoroughly implanted.

Predictable outcomes of the processes of data decomposition and article retrieval are, according to Walz and Rich: 1) synthesis and evaluation become dominant processes; 2) gaps in the information structure become evident; 3) use of impersonal resources increases; 4) opportunity for inter-professional interaction increases; 5) information, not a book, is retrieved; and 6) time to information is reduced and the band width of information is increased. The implications of data decomposition and article retrieval for pupil personnel services are: 1) the approach to learning will become that of inquiry; 2, 3, 4) the information generation process will require new skills to approach learning including stress upon the processes of evaluative integration and of information coagulation, not absorption; 5, 6) changed methods of professional communication and increased collaborative efforts will occur; and 7) small esoteric information systems will develop. Walz and Rich (1967) have thus enumerated important sets of outcomes and implications. However, their conclusion is:

> Perhaps one of the most important conclusions to be drawn from reviewing the outcomes and implications of information systems is that they may well not be a significant force for change. Wherever we have used "will", we just as well could have inserted "can". We are more assured that the mechanics of information systems are workable than we are that individuals can make the necessary changes in attitudes and beliefs to use them. The emergence of information systems is undeniably a force for change in counselor education. Whether it results in changes or not will depend upon the professional response to that force. (p.284)

Thus Walz and Rich stop somewhat short of asserting that data reduction and interactive retrieval actually will have the noted consequences. We in turn claim that the Information System for Vocational Decisions could bring data reduction and interactive retrieval into a condition where the Walz and Rich consequences actually *will* be realized, not just *can* be realized. The ISVD could itself be an interactive data reduction and retrieval system embedded within expectation, learning, and practice of personal decision-making. Decision-making was thereby to be given the role of information generator in the ISVD. Facts/data are turned into information by the inquirer within the context of decision-making *when* decision-making is subject to MONITOR, a concept we next specify.

ISVD AND MONITOR

As has been indicated, the basic scheme of ISVD was to have data files in which previously known facts/data are stored. The System would then guide personal interaction with the data files. Personal interaction would both be taught and be used in the System. Use of the System could first be as a game and then in the reality of one's own life.

MONITOR refers to the computer control functions associated with the reflexive activities required in the creation of self awareness during the decision-making practiced while choosing in using the primary data files. MONITOR was to be fashioned to operate at three levels of awareness about this reflexive activity. At the rudimentary level, vocational development, vocational maturity, and agency development theories are to be used within the paradigm of decision-making which has been outlined above. At this level, the System would itself be programmed just to assess the *quality* of decision-making as dictated by the concepts of the several theories. This would provide a first-order and mechanistic way of guarding against failures to exercise personal responsibility during the decision-making uses of the ISVD.

The second level of operation of MONITOR was to be that of giving inquirers access to the rules and procedures of the first-level MONITOR. Each time the inquirers enter the System to interact in relation to a discontinuity in their future they would be encouraged to summarize their experience in relation to prior discontinuities which they have considered in the System. This process, which was named that of REVIEW would include a routine which would create a juxtaposition of current statements about past experiences with past statements about what were then expectations about future events.

This process of comparing the formerly anticipated with the presently actual would be one of the important processes in the ISVD. The comparisons were to be processed in the ISVD by the secondary data files having to do with the generalization of decision-making into career development within the context of vocational development. This processing would require all of the procedures of heuristic meaning creation which are inherent in the ERIC system, namely 1) the provision of an original product (in the ISVD this is to be the summary of past experience which the person first supplies), 2) the abstracting of that product (in the ISVD this is to be the turning of the summary into form permitting comparison), and 3) the creation both of primary and coordinate index terms and of a thesaurus of synonyms of them. In the second level of operation of MONITOR the inquirers in ISVD were first to be instructed in our *System* use of this data reduction process which is inherent in the facilitation of heuristic meaning. The inquirers would also have to be given access to the actual procedures by which a primary and coordinate index and a thesaurus of synonyms operate in the ISVD computing system. They would then be permitted to use their own primary and coordinate index terms and thesaurus to process the summary data collected during REVIEW of their career development both at the moment and in past uses. This procedure would actually create the smaller esoteric information systems which Walz and Rich suggest within the conception of ERIC. However, within the ISVD these smaller esoteric information systems would be really personal and not accessible to another except upon authorization of an inquirer. In fact, the smaller esoteric information systems actually are the rudiments of the cognitive structure upon which each inquirer premises their personality in the realms of educational, military, vocational, and family decisions. ISVD would thus encourage the existence and applaud the formation of smaller esoteric information systems. These personal guidance systems constitute the compromises with totality which individuals must make while being accurate, detailed, and honest with themselves in an ever-maintained effort to perfect their understanding of their actions and their experience.

ISVD AND MEANING THROUGH THOUGHT, COUNSELING AND SUPERVISION

Although the substitution of this second level personal "MONITOR" information system for the original System MONITOR represents a giant step toward understanding in individuality, it does not represent the completion of the process. Completion of the process further requires the machine-free use of "MONITOR" in the practiced use of thought in experience and action. This condition is never fully attained; it is only ever more closely approximated. It requires generalization of two phases of "MONITOR." One is that of the language of "MONITOR" itself. MONITOR would necessarily be linguistic. As Dudley and Tiedeman indicate (1977), language can never be fully co-extensive with experience. Therefore, inquirers must be encouraged to see "MONITOR" as but a stage in understanding their harmonization of language and experience, not the end result itself. The end is more akin to realization of language and experience as a paradox (1967), a predicament capable of being understood and appreciated but incapable of full formal construal in co-extensive fashion.

The second part of "MONITOR" which must be generalized in reaching for a practiced ease with thought, choice, and action is the inquirers' use of the condition in a social, not just a machine, context. In short, the inquirers must move their personal "MONITOR" from machine context to interpersonal context. The counselors who supervise the inquirers discovery of their personal "MONITOR" within the interactive computer processes of the ISVD must be the first agents of generalization of "MONITOR" from machine to interpersonal context. The counselors must use their own interaction with the inquirers as laboratory for that generalization and focus their skill in the assessment and cultivation of creative processes upon the attainment of that generalization itself. Supervisors of people at school, Armed Service, or work in turn have opportunity to be the second-line agents of generalization of "MONITOR" from machine to interpersonal context. The supervisors who actually capitalize this opportunity must also use their own interaction with inquirers as laboratory for the generalization but must in turn focus their skill in assessment and cultivation of creative processes on the substance of inquirers' role obligations in the particular situation under supervision. Finally, the inquirers are themselves the ultimate agent for generalization of "MONITOR" from machine to interpersonal context. They must experience the weakness of the machine MONITOR within the context of their fantasy about control over circumstance and, with practice in machine and interpersonal contexts, gain confidence in their capacity to know some but not all of their anticipatory guiding system and its consequences in their life space.

We trust it is clear that the Information System for Vocational Decisions with its expected ramification into non-machine and personal collaborative activity could offer potential through MONITOR, "MONITOR", counseling, and supervision of turning the reduction, retrieval, and use of facts/data into an information generating function which in turn is used, understood, and appreciated. In this sense we believe that what Walz and Rich suspect only *can* happen within ERIC *will* happen within ISVD.

Despite the strength of this assertion for the information generation potential of ISVD, let no one suffer the delusion that information generation would actually occur universally. The ISVD would expect information generation to happen. The ISVD would consistently attempt to make information generation occur. The ISVD would be diagnostic about failures of information generation to appear. However, the ISVD would only actually accomplish information generation with those inquirers who both catch on to its theory and themselves come to use that theory without defense toward the System's part in its origin.

Section II

STRUCTURE AND TRANSITION[1]

PRIMARY DATA FILES OF THE ISVD

The Information System for Vocational Decisions was designed to be a system in which facts/data about educational, military, vocational and personal and family living opportunities are turned by each of its inquirers into the information of a personally-determined career. The ISVD would contain four primary data files, one for each of these kinds of opportunities. These data files would be much like the files of abstracts created for the Educational Resources Information Center (ERIC) system. Each of these four primary data files in the ISVD would be partitioned in several ways. One of these partitions would serve to distinguish between the stages of exploration or clarification in decision-making The facts/data available for an educational, military, and occupational alternative would be fewer and at a more general level for the exploratory mode than for the clarificatory mode. When exploring, inquirers would not be expected to maintain preference for an alternative. When clarifying, they would be expected either to maintain their preference for an alternative or to return to exploration. In this phase of decision making, inquirers would be expected to bring the perspective of doubt to a previously crystallized choice and to bear the anxiety of ignorance in

[1]This introduction is based on Project Report Number 12, "The Role of Decision-Making in Information Generation: An Emerging New Potential in Guidance," by David V. Tiedeman. Richard Durstine participated extensively in editing that document for this report.

the face of new facts about the chosen alternative.

A second partition of each of the primary data files would be applied within its exploratory and clarificatory parts. This partition would be according to the discontinuity, or socially induced choice situation in life for which the data file is pertinent. With the education data file, this partition would specialize according to choice of: 1) high school curriculum; 2) post-secondary institutions; 3) post-secondary specialty; 4) graduate institutions; and 5) graduate specialty. In the case of the military data file, the partition would be directed toward promotion within the enlisted and officer ranks of each of the three major U. S. Armed Services. In the case of the occupation data file, it would include the choices: 1) occupation; 2) placement; 3) promotion; and 4) career.

The occupation data file would have an adjunctive file incorporating forecasts by industry according to national and regional conditions. The primary purpose of facts/data on forecasting will be described shortly.

PURPOSE AND SELF DEVELOPMENT
THROUGH THE ISVD

The ISVD was planned to offer access to the four primary data files within the context of achieving purposeful activity during self development. Two pedagogical modes would be provided for this context. One mode would be teaching about concepts relevant to purpose in self development. The concepts included in this mode would be: 1) the psychology of becoming purposeful; 2) self and decision-making; 3) psychological attributes and educational, military, and occupational decisions; and 4) any needed instructions for use of the three primary data files.

The second pedagogical mode would be that of decision-making applied to the data both of another's life and of one's own life. The basic mode with the data of another's life could be that of a game. Inquirers either cooperate or compete with others in playing rounds in a game context that requires time planning in relation to future possibilities and consequences. The context of time planning would be in terms of education, work, leisure, and family. Future possibilities and consequences would be retrieved in part from the forecasting data file mentioned earlier. The playing of rounds of the game provides rudimentary simulation of career development. However, the ISVD would also let inquirers substitute their own data in the game structure and would then use this simulated career development structure in personal decision-making, that is in decision-making in which inquirers are themselves the players and the objects of the game. In personal decision-making, the basic andragogic mode would be that of guidance in counseling. In this mode the internalization of the game structure into the personality is expected and facilitated so that the game structure can become a guiding mechanism in the future anticipatory activity of the inquirer.

SECONDARY DATA FILES
AND ROUTINES IN THE ISVD

The substitution of one's self for the life circumstance of another would create need for two kinds of secondary files. One secondary file would be that of the individual's education and psychological characteristics. This file would be created and maintained both to permit counselors to call for cumulative records and to permit individual inquirers to generate alternative possibilities for themselves by using the predictive framework in relation to anonymous psychological characteristics, choices, and later accomplishments as based on histories of other inquirers which would be stored in this file. This technique would be augmented in the ISVD by a procedure due to Thomas Hutchinson. The Hutchinson procedure allows inquirers to specify both the alternatives under consideration and the levels of reward which they seek from each specified alternative. The procedure then provides indication of whether the inquirers' psychological data are like those of others who before them chose the alternative and achieved the designated rewards.

The secondary file would store important elements of inquirers' decisional frameworks in working out their life plans. The file would consist of summary statements which inquirers generate at the conclusion of each career, arising from using the repetitively applied routines of the ISVD in relation to each discontinuity in which they address their future and learn from their past in the ISVD. The inquirers will of course themselves be engaged in abstracting their life circumstance while creating these data for their life.

Also inherent in the secondary file on the person's decisional framework would be a procedure due to Terence J. O'Mahoney. This procedure is a paired comparison of vaguely pictured occupational activities presented to reveal the person's self concept in the context of occupational activity. Such paired comparison operations give inquirers clearer linguistic understanding of themselves in ideal and actual terms. The understanding is then an explicit basis upon which the inquirers can deepen their knowledge of their union of personality and occupation. Use of the procedure is available for the mode of exploration, not clarification. In short, the O'Mahoney procedure as expanded from its present context of just occupational pictures permits decision in an educational, military, occupational, or family context to aid in discovering harmonies and disharmonies in personal psychologies and activities.

The three Chapters in this section specify in rudimentary fashion how the ISVD was to be programmed to achieve these goals. In this regard the Section stands as a theoretical statement of what additionally needs to be done in counseling theory in order to make counseling more scientific (see Hummel, Lichtenberg, and Shaffer, 1975 for further discussion of this point).

Chapter 3

GETTING A GUIDANCE MACHINE TO UNDERSTAND ENGLISH[1]

THE CONCEPT OF THE GUIDANCE MACHINE

The first part of this section gives decision-making the role of information generator in the ISVD. It also indicates that the capacity of decision-making in information generation depended in the ISVD on the development of a guidance machine which could understand English. The guidance machine which understands English is in turn first the model and then the functioning capacity of inquirers operating in their vocational development so that their linguistic capacity to understand themselves and their career is continuously expanded.

The Section overviews the necessity for primary and secondary data files as these files are needed in the guidance machine which could understand English. In this Chapter, we therefore continue the presentation of the System which is ISVD but do so by moving from persons who are linguistically developed in their understanding of their career development to the guidance machine which had to understand English because it helped them in their linguistic development as they engaged in their vocational and career developments.

The central purpose of the ISVD was to create an environment for deciding. The needed environment must be a reckoning environment because we want inquirers to do more

---

[1] This Chapter is based on Project Report Number 14, "Getting a Guidance Machine to Understand English," by Allan B. Ellis, Margaret E. Pincus, and Patricia Yee.

than just make up their minds. We want them to figure up, measure, estimate, compare, judge, make calculated guesses, and in the end take responsibility for their decisions based in such reckonings of ours and their. This, of course, is what *deciding* means, but often people equate decision-making with choice-making and thereby miss the inherent notion of the process and its extension over time. What is left, usually, is the mistaken idea that persons decide by making up their minds, and thus we hear about the moment of decision as though it all happens at a point in time which is discrete and unbounded by thought and reflection. To make it clear that it is precisely this misconception and the resulting inflexibility we wished to challenge in ISVD, we have come to refer to the setting for vocational decision-making which we are creating as a vocational reckoning environment. However, we in turn planned to continually project in the ISVD the understanding that the reckoning people ultimately need is theirs, not ours or our machine's.

Along with the inquirers themselves there were two additional components within the ISVD reckoning environment. The first of these is an extensive collection of data about work, education, and family living. Facts about jobs, colleges, trade schools, military specialties, and about the inquirers themselves are just a few of the types of data to be stored and made available to them. These data are organized into five major data files: occupational, military, educational, personal and family living, and personal characteristics. Naturally, while each of these files is separate from the other, they all reference each other so that an inquirer may follow a question through all its aspects.

An important point which ISVD wants the inquirer to realize about data is that in the real world they are never complete. Often it is precisely this incompleteness of data about the world of work that makes decisions necessary in the first place. Thus, before one begins the process of decision-making one must understand the incompleteness of the data with which one is dealing. (Ellis and Wetherell, 1966).

The result we hoped for is that by developing these skills the inquirers would cultivate in themselves a *sense of agency*, that is, the belief that they are the significant agents in determining what happens to them.

Between the inquirer and the data we intended to place a guidance machine. The function of this third and final element of the ISVD reckoning environment was to be to facilitate inquirers access to data and vice versa. That is, not only did we wish to provide a means for inquirers to gain convenient access to data, but we wished to keep track of such access as well. In this way, not only could individuals get facts with which to make decisions, but they could also gain a sense of the way they go about making decisions.

One way, then, to describe the vocational reckoning environment of ISVD is shown in this diagram:

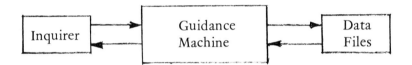

There is, of course, no such thing as a guidance machine, and the major task of ISVD, therefore, was to be to build one. Instead of building this machine in the usual way with pliers and screwdriver, however, ISVD was planned to transform an existing computer into a guidance machine by programming its software in appropriate ways and by inserting the materials called for by that software.

Software programming and new material construction are not unnatural tasks in a computing project, since computers are made for this sort of thing. What most people call a computer program is in fact an explicit statement of a procedure, and at the same time a description of the machine needed to perform that procedure. This is a behavioral description, but it is all that a computer needs in order to imitate the machine so described. It was to be the purpose of ISVD, therefore, to create a sufficiently explicit description of the behavior of a guidance machine so that a computer could behave as though it were that machine.

Our efforts to create a description of a guidance machine fell into two categories. The first was the development of certain necessary software. This consisted of a fairly elaborate set of computer programs which permit certain basic and generally required functions to be performed. We needed, for example, to operate in a time-shared setting so that more than one person could use the system at any one time. Furthermore, we had to provide the ability to create, maintain, edit, and retrieve data files. A programming language to allow both string manipulation and list processing, programs for statistical analyses, routines to permit content analysis, and the general facility of keeping track of who is on the system and what needs to be done next are some other examples of the kind of necessary computer software with which we were concerned.

The second category of a description of a guidance machine was the ISVD software itself. These are the programs that enable our time-shared computer to behave like a guidance machine, and it is here that any substantive contributions of ISVD rest.

The single, most significant component of the ISVD software is that network of routines we called *scripts*. Not unlike the manuscript of a play (from which it gets its name) a script is a set of rules describing how the guidance machine is to act. Scripts contain such things as the text to be presented to a person via either a video display device or a printer, commands to activate a tape recorder, or motion picture projector or to display a 35mm slide, instructions for how to process the inquirers' responses, and rules for any computation or storage or retrieval of data.

When an inquirer interacts with a guidance machine under control of our scripts, the inquirer will write a *scenario*. A scenario is the record of the inquirer's personal dialogue in the "play" which was our script. A scenario is illustrated later in this Chapter.

We believed that a major feature of scripts must be the ability to allow what appears to be conversation between an individual and the guidance machine, because so much of the process of deciding consists of unstructured behavior (such as browsing through data files). Thus, inquirers must be free enough to generate their own questions and the resulting scenario in as natural a form as possible. To this end we spent some time in exploring the problem of getting a computer to seem to understand and to respond to English questions posed by the inquirer.

THE OPERATION OF A GUIDANCE MACHINE

There have been a number of efforts to get computers to deal with English sentences. Among these the works of Bobrow (1963), Green, Chomsky, Laughery, and Wolf (1961), Helm (1965), Simmons (1962), and Stone, Dunphy, Smith, and Ogilvie (1966) are especially relevant to ISVD. While we carefully examined the work of all these men to determine how we might benefit from them, this section is confined to but one such line of work. Specifically, we will describe our effort to adapt to our needs the computer program called ELIZA developed by Joseph Weizenbaum (1963) of the Massachusetts Institute of Technology.

While ELIZA is a computer program, it is convenient to think of it more as a scriptwriting language (Weizenbaum 1966, 1967). The language permits an author to specify certain kinds of natural language conversations between man and machine. The ELIZA program accepts as input, scripts which describe the nature of the desired interaction. It is the job of the main program to process these scripts.

An ELIZA script is divided into two parts: a keyword section and a program section. The keyword section contains keywords and decomposition and reassembly rules. As Taylor (1967) indicates, "The keywords provide some hint as to what the student is talking about while decomposition rules provide a way to analyze his sentence to determine what he is saying." The reassembly rules describe how the program is to fashion a response to the user's input, while the program part of the script contains further details of what is to be done when there is a match between a decomposition rule and an inputted sentence.

Specifying keywords is particularly important in ELIZA and entails not only constructing a relevant set of such words but also requires a concern for their position in an input sentence. Consider, for example, one possible response to the question,

What would you like to do today?

I want to play the game of baseball with you.

This sentence matches the decomposition rule:

(0 (*play take use see try) 0 game 0)

GAME is an important keyword in this script since it connotes an important part of the ISVD system. In the above example the machine has "recognized" the fact that the inquirer would like to play a game, but it does not know which one since the word baseball was not picked up. The decomposition rule is very general and will probably match many different inputted sentences. Since this is the case, it must transfer control to a general statement which says:

Within the ISVD system there are only two kinds of games that you can play. One is called the life career game and one is a risk taking game. Which one do you want?

Rather tactfully, it reminds inquirers that in order " to play" the system they must stay within its context. Now consider the following:

I want to play the life career game.

---

*(Meaning: any number of words, including no words at all, followed by one of the words in parentheses, followed by any number of words, followed by the word game, followed by any number of words.)

The above decomposition rule would match this input as well but the response would be inappropriate. So we must make a more specific rule:

(0 (*play take use see try) 0 life career game 0)

and the transfer is directly to the game.

However, what if the inquirers had said:

I certainly do not want to play the life career game

This sentence would match the above decomposition rule and transfer directly to the game, which, of course, would be an inappropriate response. So we must provide another decomposition rule that would provide for the negative:

(0 not (*play take use see try) 0 life career game 0)

Obviously then, the only way that we could be absolutely sure that the machine would understand what the inquirer is saying is to specify all the alternative decomposition rules with a particular keyword—probably an almost impossible task! How many ways can one use the word game in a sentence? How many and what words could possibly precede and follow it? The best we can do is to create our decomposition rules based on a confidence level of expected student response.

Although we will always as scientists do the best we can in specifying key-words, decomposition rules and reconstitution principles, we pause here to note the particularly important fact that *it is this very impossibility for completeness in the English understanding of the guidance machine which makes the guidance machine appropriate to the theory of the ISVD.* The theory of ISVD calls for inquirers to interact with the System until they are satisfied that they can operate with its linguistic understanding but without need for later reference to it except for the help which they can always get from its data files and their esoteric infromation system. Because the guidance machine will invariably have incompleteness in its key-words, decomposition rules, and reconstitution principles, inquirers will eventually find that the guidance machine cannot understand the English which they elect to use. The appearance of these times constitute teachable moments in the ISVD. The inquirers can either then go away mad and forever damn the machine because it cannot do what they expected it to do for them or they can then go back into the sequence they were pursuing and find out where the sequence began to fail with our key-words, decomposition rules and reconstitution principles. With MONITOR the inquirers will additionally be able to reprogram their own data file so that failures disturbing to them do not later occur. In that process, the inquirers will be learning that career is in them and that capability and confidence in working with career conceptions can be theirs if they but make some of our language theirs.

Returning then to our story about the operation of a guidance machine itself, decomposition rules in an ELIZA script are listed in order of generality, the most specific listed first, and so on. The following is an example of the keyword section in our ORIENTATION script for the word "game," specifically the rules of play:

(game (game (−specification of keyword

(0 how 0 (*play take use see try) 0 risk 0 game 0) ()aaa

(0 how 0 (*play take use see try) 0 life career game 0) ()bb

(0 rules 0 life career game 0) ()bb

(0 rules 0 risk game 0) ()aaa

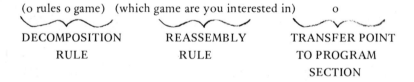

(o rules o game)	(which game are you interested in)	o
DECOMPOSITION RULE	REASSEMBLY RULE	TRANSFER POINT TO PROGRAM SECTION

Aside from keywords, decomposition and recomposition rules, ELIZA operates on several other powerful mehcanisms.

The first of these is called a DLIST. This function allows the scriptwriter to tag certain words as belonging to a particular category. Consider the following:

(MOTHER DLIST (/FAMILY))

(FATHER DLIST (/FAMILY))

(BROTHER DLIST (/FAMILY))

(SISTER DLIST (/FAMILY))

Mother, father, brother, and sister are all tagged family. This saves considerable time in decomposition rules. Instead of specifying a decompostion rule for each word, the scriptwriter can do the following:

(O LOVE 0 (/FAMILY) 0)

which means: match an inputted sentence that has any number of words, followed by the word LOVE, followed by any number of words, followed by any word tagged FAMILY, followed by any number of words.

Now a reassembly rule would allow the computer to come back with an appropriate response:

(0 LOVE 0 (/FAMILY) 0) (WHY DO YOU LOVE YOUR 4.)

The 4 refers to the fourth element in the decomposition rule. In this case, the word tagged family. A conversation could go like this:

S: I love my mother.

C: Why do you love your mother.

S: Because she's nice to me.

C: Do any other reasons come to mind.
(This response is triggered by the word "because.")

Another important mechanism is the ability to make substitutions in the inquirer's input and then apply decomposition rules to the revised input. For instance, some of the substitutions that we made were:

(OF COURSE = YES.)

(YEAH = YES.)

(NATURALLY = YES.)

(RIGHT = YES.)

What happens then is that any time "of course," "yeah," "naturally," or "right" occur in the input, the computer substitutes the word "YES." If we are looking for YES responses from users and they type in any of the above, their input would then be treated as a YES.

A third mechanism is known as the table mechanism. This is powerful because it keeps track of the context of the conversation. It is used when there is a possibility of several different user responses, each of which refers to a previous context. For instance, a user might answer a question YES, NO, or UNSURE. In the key-word section of the script we have the following:

(0 YES 0 DLIST (YYY))

(0 NO 0 DLIST (NNN))

(0 (/UNSURE) 0 DLIST (ZZZ))

Each decomposition rule is given a tag; the first is tagged (YYY), the second (NNN), and the third (ZZZ).

In the program section following the question, is the table.
*A TYPE ('DO YOU LIKE TO PLAY GAMES.'), NEWTOP ('YYY AA NNN AB ZZZ AC O'E M), TABLE).

The instructions to the computer go as follows:

TYPE the sentence 'DO YOU LIKE TO PLAY GAMES.' If the answer is "yes" go to the label (another piece of text usually) AA; if the answer is "no" go to the label AB; if the answer is a word tagged "unsure" go to the label AC; otherwise (O'E) go to the label M. STOP, wait for input (indicated by the period following the last parenthesis).

Another important feature of ELIZA is the ability of one

script to call into play another script, to switch control and to return to the main script when that level of conversation has been terminated. We made heavy use of this ability. For a more complete description of ELIZA, refer to the work of Taylor (1967) and Hayward (1968).

ORIENTATION, ACCESS ROUTINES AND A SCENARIO IN ISVD: AN ILLUSTRATION OF AN INQUIRER INTER-ACTING WITH FILES THROUGH ORIENTATION AND ROUTINES PROGRAMMED IN ELIZA

Access Routines and the Orientation Script in ISVD

Stated simply, our first task in creating a guidance machine was to experiment with ELIZA in order to demonstrate its usefulness to the ISVD. We accomplished this task in the writing of demonstration scripts for the Access Routines of EXPLORATION and CLARIFICATION as well as for the ISVD ORIENTATION.

An access routine is a set of scripts that allow an inquirer access to various scripts, procedures, and to one or more of the System's several data files. In the ISVD, they are named EXPLORATION, CLARIFICATION, and REVIEW in an effort to use names close to the conditions in the Tiedeman-O'Hara paradigm of decision-making. The theory of access routine REVIEW was described in Chapter 2. EXPLORA-TION and CLARIFICATION are merely exemplified in this section as they operated as scripts which in turn gave rise, because of inquirer interaction to an inquirer's scenario.

Our scripts used in this experiment were inherently different from those developed elsewhere for the System in that they served as calling (access) scripts or as data collection scripts. The purpose of a calling script is to ascertain what inquirers want to do: do they want to access the occupation data base, play the Life Career Game, developed by Sarane Boocock (1967), or think about which colleges to apply to? After the script has determined what it is that the inquirer wants, it calls in the appropriate materials.

A data collection script, on the other hand, asks for specific information from the inquirer (e.g. what factors are important to you in thinking about college choice?), then analyzes the information and stores it for later use in the System.

In the demonstration ELIZA ISVD script system, the ORIENTATION script was used in 1966 as the main calling script. The keywords in this script referred to our three then operable primary data files (occupations, military, and education), and to the Life Career Game.

Inquirers as they went through the ISVD ORIENTATION script may or may not know what they want to do in the System. If the latter is the case, control was transferred to a script designed to help them choose an activity by checking their personal data file for suggestions.

In the following example of a possible interaction the computer's output is in san serif type, and the inquirer's input is in serif type.

What would you like to do today?

I don't know.

Have you thought about what courses you are going to take next year?

Yes.

Would you like to explore that further now?

No.

Well, have you thought about what you would like to do after you graduate from high school?

Yes, I want to go to college.

Would you like to talk about college choice?

O.K.

Fine. Since we know that you have not explored your college choice with the System before, the first thing we would like to find out is if you have thought about this choice enough to have some alternatives in mind. If you do, type the names of each of the alternative colleges. If not, type in the word no. After an activity has been selected (in this case, college choice) control would be transferred to one of the access routine's scripts.

If we think of the ISVD as a network of scripts, then inquirers were given a choice of three different kinds of scripts:

1) they could declare themselves ignorant of vocationally relevant concepts and thereby gain access to concept teaching scripts;

2) if they realize that future decisions affect that life (plan, style, etc.) and they want to find out how, they could elect scripts for practice (such as the game);

3) if they want to play the game for "real," using their own data and applying 1 and 2, they could gain access to the decision-making access routines (EXPLORATION, CLARIFICATION, and REVIEW).

In the Tiedeman-O'Hara paradigm of decision-making, the purpose of exploration is to generate alternatives. Activity is to be planned so that alternatives are selected and so that preferences start to form. After an inquirer has explored any number of alternatives, crystallization should produce preferred alternatives and the bases on which those alternatives are favored. The purpose of the CLARIFICATION access routine was to test how strongly individuals maintained their commitment. Major activities in the routine were 1) those that determine if the bases for crystallization and choice do in fact exist and that the individual is aware of them, and 2) those activities that determine if these bases are realistically sound or too inhibitive.

The access routines must allow inquirers to vacillate between EXPLORATION and CLARIFICATION when an alternative comes to mind, is only partially pursued, and is augmented by another alternative which in turn is only partially pursued. The repetition of these pursuits must be programmed so that they somehow give rise to a superordinate structure in which inquirers can see crystallization and evoke the belief that they have chosen.

Since our intention was first to create a demonstration of ELIZA's capabilities we did not complete all the scripts that these access routines require. We feel satisfied, nonetheless, that the capabilities of ELIZA would have allowed us to come close to reflecting the Tiedeman-O'Hara paradigm of decision-making.

**A Scenario in ISVD Using the
ELIZA Experimental Programs**

The following extended example of an inquirer's interaction with the ISVD EXPLORATION and CLARIFICATION scripts will serve to indicate the ways in which ELIZA was being applied to our problem. We provide such a lengthy example to suggest not only the capabilities of our demonstration system but also to provide a sense of the kind of flexibility we wished to offer the inquirer. In the scenario which follows,[2] the computer's output is once again in san serif type; the inquirer's input in serif type.

What would you like to do today.

I want to think about colleges to apply to next year.

Since we know that you have not explored your college choice with the System before, the first thing we would like to find out is if you have thought about this choice enough to have some alternatives in mind. If you do, type the names of each of the alternative colleges. If not, type in the word no.

Harvard University, Boston College, and Berkeley.

---

[2] Because this demonstration was created roughly to explore technical, not substantive problems, the content or the wording of the scripts was subject to change as we implemented the intent of the grant. Bear in mind also that all data in this script were correct in 1967 but may no longer be so in 1978.

Good. What kinds of things did you do in exploring college choice. Did you read any college catalogues or talk with your guidance counselor. Make as complete a statement as possible.

I read the catalogue for Harvard and Boston College. I talked to my guidance counselor, and had a couple of interviews with the Dean at Harvard. My father went to Berkeley so that's why I'm interested in going there.

These are the activities the machine has recognized or analyzed from your statement. You have discussed the matter with members of the family, spoken with a guidance counselor, read some college catalogues, spoken with college officials. Here are some other things that may be a good idea to do if you haven't already. You could have discussed the matter with a teacher. Now then, look at the list of exploration activities that you performed outside of the System. Here is the list of your present alternatives.

Harvard University, Boston College, and Berkeley. Now type in the activities that you feel helped you most in making up your mind or gave you some alternative colleges to think about. Please type them in in order of importance.

The interviews and talking with my Dad.

Good. Before we go on to explore college choice, what are the factors that you think are important in considering which colleges to apply to.

Grades, class rank.

Anything else.

Tuition costs, test scores.

Here are some of the factors that other students found important (1) curriculum choice (2) course selection (high school subjects) (3) grades (4) class rank (5) test scores (PSAT SAT, CEEB, ACT) (6) extra-curricular activities (7) future vocational plans (8) goal in going to college (9) post college education and/or training.

Here is your list. Grades, class rank, tuition costs, test scores. Look at both lists and then type in all factors from both lists that you consider important in thinking about college choice.

High school courses, grades, class rank, test scores, tuition costs, future vocational plans.

Fine. There are several ways that you can go about thinking about college choice within the ISVD system. You can go through some concept scripts which are designed to give you some facts on topics relevant to college choice. Or you can play the life career game. Using the data of a make believe student who is like you in some ways you go through the process of selecting a college for that student. If you have specific colleges in mind, you can get data on them by accessing the education data file.

If you like, you can let the System guide you through a statement of preferences to come up with a list of colleges that most nearly matches your preferences. Or you can elect to first go through a unit on decision-making, a unit that tries to help you understand yourself and others in relation to making decisions. What would you like to do.

Access the education data file.

You have access to the education data file. For demonstration purposes only, the following schools have been implemented. Harvard College (men), Goucher College (women), Berkeley University (large state supported school), Boston College (religiously affiliated), and Carnegie Institute (technical training school);

The following four variables have been implemented . . . costs (including tuition, room and board, and other fees), required entrance exams, criteria used in selecting students and required high school courses.

Now then you can query this micro data base in any way that you want. Please do not use question marks. If you wish to stop at any time, type in the word stop.

54   CAREER DEVELOPMENT

You may begin.

How much does it cost to go to Harvard.

Tuition at Harvard is 2000 dollars per year including lab and health fees. Room and board is 1170 dollars. Non-resident student fee is 25 dollars. Books and supplies about 70 dollars per year. Personal expenses about 375 dollars including room supplies, clothing, cleaning and laundry, recreation, and other personal expenses (except travel).

How does that compare with Boston College.

Boston College's tuition is 1600 dollars, room and board is 1050 dollars. Other costs include books and supplies about 100 dollars, lab fee 100 dollars and 30 dollars for women boarding students for health fees.

What high school courses should I take for Boston College.

No specific number of units is required. However, the following minimum is required . . . English (4), algebra (2), plane geometry (1), foreign language (2), trigonometry (for students planning to major in math), biology, chemistry or physics (2 for students planning to major in the above sciences and for applicants to the school of nursing), academic electives (5).

What specific entrance exams are required.

Boston College requires the SAT and three achievement tests. English, level I or II mathematics, and one of the candidate's choice.

Does Berkeley require the SAT.

Applicants who are ineligible, due to grade average, or to unit or distribution deficiencies, or who have graduated from an unaccredited secondary school, may qualify for admission by CEEB examinations. The three achievement tests required for those applying for admission are . . . English, one test in social studies or foreign language, one test in mathematics or a science. Requirements for California residents . . . total SAT

DESIGNING OUR CAREER MACHINES 55

score of at least 1000, and total score on three ACH of at least 1650 with no single ACH less that 500.0. Requirements for out-of-state residents . . . total SAT score of at least 1100 and total score on three ACH of at least 1725.0.

What are the costs there.

Tuition at Berkeley is 980 dollars per year of three quarters for out-of-state students. No tuition for California residents. Room and board varies between 600 and 940 dollars. Incidental fee of 242 dollars. Associated students membership fee 11 dollars. Books and supplies about 80 to 110 dollars.

How do they choose their students.

Harvard chooses its candidates on the following criteria. Secondary school record, school's recommendation, and CEEB scores. Also, character, personality and extracurricular participation are strongly emphasized. Special talents and interests also considered.

How much does it cost to go to Goucher.

There is a comprehensive fee of 2950 dollars per year including tuition, room and board, and lab fees. Student activity fee of 13 dollars, health fee 50 dollars, and gymnasium outfit 27 dollars. Other costs include books and supplies about 100 dollars.

What kinds of courses should I take.

16 units required, the following recommended . . . English (4), mathematics (3), (2 in Algebra, 1 in Geometry), one foreign language (3), History (2), Laboratory Science (1). The committee on admissions may allow entrance credit for work in elective subjects not listed.

How do they pick their students.

Goucher College bases its candidate selection on the secondary school record, the school's recommendation, and test scores. Other important factors are personal characteristics, extracurricular participation, and individual interests. Alumnae relationships and geographical distribution considered.

I think I would like to stop now.

Would you like a summary of your exploration of the education data file.

Yes.

Fine. You got data on the following variables for Harvard College . . . Costs, including tuition and room and board, how the school selects its students.

For Boston College you got data on the following variables. . . Costs, including tuition and room and board, what high school course are recommended or required for entrance, what admissions tests you should take.

You have found out about what admissions tests you should take, costs, including tuition and room and board, how the school selects its students, for the University of California at Berkeley.

For Goucher College you explored the data on the following variables . . . Costs, including tuition and room and board, what high school courses are recommended or required for entrance, how the school selects its students.

You didn't explore the available data on Carnegie Institute. Now then, Would you like to go back and find out anything more about these schools.

No.

Would you like to go into clarification now.

Yes.

Of the following colleges that you have explored, which would you consider applying to.

Harvard University, University of California at Berkeley, Boston College, Goucher College.

Boston College, maybe Berkeley, and Harvard.

DESIGNING OUR CAREER MACHINIES   57

Are they listed in order of preference, that is, is your first choice first, etc.

No.

Please type them in order of preference.

Harvard University, Boston College, Berkeley.

You have decided to go into clarification concerning your preferred alternative Harvard University.

You have accessed the education data base and gotten some of the available data on Harvard University.

In exploration, you stated that you considered the following to be important factors in considering college choice . . . grades, class rank, test scores, course, goal.

Now then, you should have a fairly good idea of where you stand in relation to these factors as well as where students admitted to Harvard University stand. Right.

No.

Would you like to go back to exploration to find out how you compare with Harvard students.

No.

Would you like to choose another activity.

Sure.

What would you like to do.

Find out about jobs.

How would you like to do this.

I would like to access the occupation data base.

O.K. This occupation information script is an example of how specific information can be extracted from the civilian occupation data base. For this script, the following five jobs were selected—doctor, lawyer, barber, machinist, and musician. Seven categories of information are provided for each title—a description of job duties, salary, beneficial high school courses, educational requirements, working hours, future demand, and percentage of men and women in field. If at any time you wish to stop, type the word stop. You may now begin.

Tell me about the work of a doctor.

Doctors are professionals who work in medical services, government, and colleges and universities. Their work is scientific and technical, and involves them with people. On the job they diagnose, and prescribe medication for diseases, treat injuries, and do surgery.

What is the salary.

Beginning doctors can expect to make at least $6500 per year, and may eventually make a maximum of $70,000 per year. Since many doctors are self-employed, they can sometimes set the number of hours they wish to work and therefore vary their income.

How many men are there in this profession.

70 to 95% of all doctors are men.

What are their working hours.

Doctors often work nights and weekends. Doctors sometimes work outdoors.

Describe their education.

Doctors must complete professional or graduate school before entering their occupation. They need four to ten years of specific training for the job and then six months to one year of on-the-job training before being considered a full-fledged doctor.

How long do doctors live on the average.

Unfortunately there is nothing for that subject. Would you like to know the topics of information that are available for doctors.

Yes.

For a doctor there is information about what they do on their job, their education, advancement, applicable high school courses, salary, necessary abilities, physical demands of the job, future growth of the profession, percentage who are men, hours, licensing requirements, and working conditions. Would you like to see one of these topics.

Yes.

What is it.

What will be the need for doctors.

Current information indicates that in the future there will be an increasing demand for doctors.

What high school courses would it be helpful to take to become a doctor.

A high school student interested in becoming a doctor should consider taking the following courses—biology, Latin, chemistry, foreign languages, physics, and social studies.

For a lawyer.

A high school student interested in becoming a lawyer should consider taking the following courses—business, Latin, English, history, speech, and social studies.

What about the pay.

Beginning lawyers should expect to make at least $5500 per year. In addition they may receive health and life insurance and paid vacations. Since lawyers may be self-employed, they can sometimes set the number of hours they wish to work and therefore vary their income.

What about a barber.

Beginning barbers should expect to make at least $65 per week, and may eventually make a maximum of $200 per week. In addition they may receive tips and health and life insurance and paid vacations. Since barbers may be self-employed, they can sometimes set the number of hours they wish to work and therefore vary their income.

And machinists.

They may receive free advanced training, overtime pay, and health and life insurance and paid vacations. Since machinists may be self-employed, they can sometimes set the number of hours they wish to work and therefore vary their income.

Describe the work.

Machinists are machine workers in the manufacturing of metal products, the manufacturing of electrical machinery, utility companies and the manufacturing of machinery. Their work requires them to deal with machines and techniques. On the job they set up and operate machine tools to make or repair metal parts or products.

Tell me about musicians.

Musicians are professionals who work in special schools, dance halls and schools and theaters, orchestras, and clubs. Their work is abstract and creative and requires them to deal with people and ideas rather than with things and objects. On the job they entertain the public by playing in symphony orchestras, dance bands, or jazz combos.

What kind of education do they need.

Musicians must complete high school and should also graduate from college before entering their occupation. They need four to ten years of specific training for the job before being considered a full-fledged musician.

Stop.

Would you like a summary of your exploration of the occupation data base.

No.

Do you want to go into clarification.

No.

What would you like to do.

I would like to access the military data file.

In the ISVD military data file you may see specific information for the Army, Navy, Air Force and general information for officers and enlisted men. You may use the military selection script and let the computer sort out jobs which may be of interest to you, or you may request descriptions for specific military jobs. What do you wish to do.

Take the job selection script.

The Navy, Army, and Air Force each have hundreds of specialized jobs. In order to simplify classification, these have been categorized by function according to career fields. The information presented here for each career field covers the various specialized positions included within it. Although not all of the general information given will apply for each specialty, you will receive an overview of the career field. To determine which career fields are best suited to you, it will help for you to answer the following questions. Armed forces jobs are performed in many locations. Indicate where you would prefer to work by selection one or more of the choices from the following list.

1. On land
2. At sea
3. In the air
4. Indoors
5. Outdoors

(Note—For this demonstration, only the first question of the military job selection script is shown. After inquirers have finished with this segment of activities, they will be queried as to whether they wish to continue with the Military Data Base).

Are you interested in seeing other things in the military data file.

Yes.

And what would you like to do next.

What is there to do.

You may look at job descriptions or request specific information for the Army, Navy, Air Force, officers and enlisted personnel.

Let me see information about the Army.

What do you wish to explore in the Army data file.

What about pay.

Here is the pay scale for enlisted men. Enlistees qualify for pay grades E-1 through E-9.

Minimum Time in Grade for Advancement	Grade	Minimum Monthly Pay	Maximum Monthly Pay
E-1 to E-2 4 months	E-1	$ 90.60	$129.00 a month after 2 yrs. total service
E-2 to E-3 6 months	E-2	100.50	141.00 a month after 2 yrs. total service
E-3 to E-4 6 months	E-3	121.80	193.80 a month after 4 yrs. total service
E-4 to E-5 1 year	E-4	168.60	252.60 a month after 6 yrs. total service
E-5 to E-6 2 years	E-5	200.40	328.80 a month after 14 yrs. total service
E-6 to E-7 3 years	E-6	232.20	387.60 a month after 18 yrs. total service
E-7 to E-8 3 years	E-7	269.40	528.60 a month after 30 yrs. total service
E-8 to E-9 2 years	E-8	428.40	587.10 a month after 26 yrs. total service
	E-9	510.60	657.30 a month after 26 yrs. total service

Here is the pay scale for commissioned officers.

Rank: Air Force and Army	Navy	Monthly Pay: Normal Minimum	Monthly Pay: Normal Maximum
Second Lieutenant	Ensign	$ 303.90	$ 336.30
First Lieutenant	Lieutenant Jr. Grade	420.30	504.60
Captain	Lieutenant	583.20	633.30
Major	Lt. Commander	700.50	807.30
Lt. Colonel	Commander	930.60	992.40
Colonel	Captain	1121.40	1216.50
Brigadier General	Rear Admiral (Lower Half)	1295.10	1384.80
Major General	Rear Admiral (Upper Half)	1530.60	1592.40
Lt. General	Vice Admiral	1648.20	1766.10
General	Admiral	1883.70	2002.60

Is there another subject in the Army Data File that you would like to see.

What topics are left.

There are nine general categories of information in the Army Data File—pay and benefits, education and training, special units, women in the Army, promotion, enlistment requirements, the reserve program, and officer status for enlisted personnel. If you are interested in finding out what Army or military jobs may be suitable for you request the job selection script. What topic or subject would you like to investigate.

What about officers.

One can achieve commisioned officer status by enrolling

at a civilian college or university for a bachelor's degree or by appointment to the U.S. Military Academy or Officer Candidate School. Upon completion of any of these programs, one is commissioned as a Reserve Second Lieutenant. What else interests you.

I don't want to continue.

Are you interested in seeing other things in the Military Data File.

No.

Here are activities that may be of interest to you. You can learn about yourself by studying how you make decisions. You can play games which give you practice in planning educational and vocational activities. You may also work with the education and occupation data files. Do you wish to look at decision making scripts, play a game, or work with the education or occupation data files.

Play a game.

In the ISVD there are two kinds of games you can play. One gives you practice in taking risks. The other gives you practice in planning educational and vocational activities. What kind of game would you like to play.

The second kind.

The life career game is designed to give you practice in forming your educational and vocational plans. Since you have never played the game with the System before, it might be wise to go through a general orientation. Do you want to do this.

Why not.

Think hard now. What was the first game you ever played.

Tag.

Do you remember how much you liked it.

Yeah.

Why did you enjoy playing tag.

It was a blast.

As children we like to play games such as tag, marbles, hop-scotch, tic-tac-toe, and hide-n-go-seek because they are fun. These games allow us to compete with other kids to try and win. But we can't say that they really teach us anything that is directly applicable to events in real life. Some games in addition to being fun, teach us something about real life activities. Have you ever played a game that seemed to be teaching you something about what goes on in real life.

Of course.

Well, games like Monopoly, Big Business, and Risk do teach us about things in real life (like buying and selling real estate, etc.). We call such games simulations.

The life career game is such a simulation. What you can learn from this game is the kind of planning that involves making decisions about things that are happening now at the same time you are thinking ahead to what you might want in the future. What kinds of decisions are you thinking about now that will have an effect on your future.

I do not wish to continue.

Are you interested in doing something else.

No, I would like to stop.

You have just exited from the System. Goodby.

Chapter 4

DATA FILES FOR COMPUTERIZED VOCATIONAL GUIDANCE: REQUIREMENTS, PREPARATION, USE[1]

THE CONCEPT OF DATA FILES

The first part of this section laid out the role which decision-making is given as information generator in ISVD. Through ISVD, inquirers would be helped to bring their vocational and career developments to an integrated condition of subvocalization. The ISVD would bring the linquistic structure of people's career development ever further to the fore of their personal attention. The guidance machine which understands English is the prime mechanism for this goal. A guidance machine which can be taught to understand English has been described in Chapter 3.

The guidance machine which understands English would have the capacity through access routines either of responding to direct inquiry or of sending the inquirer to any one of the numerous data files which could be available through command of the programs of the guidance machine. The conception of data files is one which had to be developed specifically for the guidance machine which lurks in the Information System for Vocational Decisions. Hence we describe here the specific theory of data files since that theory underlies many of the activities which are reported in the next section.

The project since its beginning embodied the concept of large, orderly collections of factual information as an impor-

[1] This Chapter is based on Project Report Number 15, "Datafiles for Computerized Vocational Guidance: Requirements, Preparation, and Use," by Richard M. Durstine.

tant part of its resources. This led to the acquisition of several such collections of information (data files). It also led to some general understandings about collection, storage, processing, and use of information for computerized guidance. These were developed and tested to the extent that a unified discussion of them is possible.

We present and explain here the approach to computer-managed information that was thus arrived at, treating theory and related action, both past and planned.

Throughout we seek consistency with related theory and activities of the ISVD. Innocence of guidance and of computer technology may cause some errors in these areas, though we hope not to the extent of invalidating the major points of the theory of data files. These major points are:

1. Data should be collected and presented specifically to aid students in their vocational decisions.

2. Data should be treated in a form that exploits high speed computation. It hence needs to be systematic and highly structured.

3. The power and flexibility of operation thus gained is worth the price of rigidity of structure.

4. For the present, accuracy is of importance secondary to that of operational design.

5. Ready-made sources of information should be relied upon as far as possible. Direct collection of information is costly.

6. It is important (and possible) to articulate data from distinct and diverse sources into a working whole.

7. A primitive form of mediation between "facts/data" and "information" should be included with the data files.

8. Data files and means of access to them should be prepared separate from one another so they can be used in a variety of combinations.

9. The information given by the system should be suggestive, not prescriptive. It is the inquirer's responsibility to know and make use of this fact.

Some more specific criteria and general rules for their implementation will be found at the end of the Chapter. The intervening discussion supports and elaborates on these general statements, drawing support mainly from the experience of preparing data files of occupational and military information for the ISVD.

THE FUNDAMENTAL TASK
IN PREPARATION OF DATA FILES

The intended role of factual information in the ISVD implies two special requirements:

1. It should be collected, analyzed, and presented specifically to aid inquirers in their vocational decisions.

2. It should be treated in a form that exploits the resources of high speed computation. It needs hence to be systematic and highly structured.

Each of these points is perhaps more significant than it looks.

Much factual information of possible value in personal decisions, particularly occupational decisions, is not generally found in useful form. It tends to be better suited for economists, planners, and employers. It needs special interpretation for profitable use by individuals. The psychology of occupations as it has developed is a step in this direction. Also needed is modification of highly detailed information to a form that serves the individual. This was the direction of the work described here.

Second, the need to deal with very large quantities of information concurrently, in many combinations and for many purposes, imposes strict requirements on treatment of that information. Also, a working vocational information system should accept with minimum disruption changes or additions to the information it treats or uses. Both these needs lead to involvement of the computer and demand a highly structured system. This degree of structure is the price of size and flexibility. We conjecture that the benefit is often worth that price.

It is certainly a possibility worth exploring.

The structure thus imposed on factual information within the ISVD led to the objection that the result may be "too mechanical." But this is functional and necessary to the approach we were taking. To cover it up would be troublesome and misleading. To eliminate it would for a long time to come be inefficient and costly. To be openly mechanical in this is a simple matter of honesty. A computerized information system that pretends to be fully human has no more self-evident merit than an airplane with flapping wings or a telephone with moveable lips at the earpiece.

A DATA FILE AND HOW IT GREW

The development of data files within the ISVD began with preparation and use of the project's first data file in the academic year 1966-67. A brief description of this file will motivate some of the conclusions that have been subsequently reached concerning data files in general.

The first data file will be referred to here as the "850 Titles File." It contained infromation under fifty-six categories about some 850 occupational titles. The categories are shown in Appendix I. This title-category structure is useful—and obvious—one for data files in general. To render this concept explicit, an illustrative "mini-data file" is shown in Figure 1.

FIGURE 1

Illustrative Short Data File Based
on Occupational Titles

Title	D.O.T. Number	Coded Data	Descriptive Information
Forest Engineer	005.187	45 0 5 1	Designs and Oversees Construction of Facilities for Logging
Egg Breaker	521.887	4 1 2 9	Separates Eggs for Use in Food Products

This tiny illustrative file gives a brief verbal description of the activities of workers in each of two occupations. In addition, in coded form, are given:

1. *Dictionary of Occupational Titles (D.O.T.)* number of the occupation;

2. Working conditions (first two columns under *Coded Data*);

3. Education required (third column under *Coded Data*);

4. Seasonality of work (fourth column under *Coded Data*).

For example, the code "45" indicates that forest engineers must use their hands, and be able to speak and hear to work. Egg breakers, on the other hand, also work with their hands, but need not speak or hear. This information is contained in the position and identity of the letters and numbers in the file. Hence great care is required in designing the data file to transmit precisely the intended meaning.

The illustrative data file also tells that a forest engineer works out of doors (an "O" in an assigned position of the file carries this information), while an egg breaker works indoors (indicated by an "I" in like position). Likewise a "5" and a "2," appropriately placed, indicate the levels of general education required for each (some college for the forest engineer, and some high school for the egg breaker). Finally, in the last column of code, a "1" indicates some seasonality in the engineer's work. "9" shows no information on this for the egg breaker.

This illustrative file exhibits all the characteristics and uses associated with any data file of this form. Though the 850 Titles File required sixteen punched cards for the coded and other information about each title, it and the illustrative file are identical in their essential characteristics.

The mechanics of construction of a data file in this form are simple but strict. The way in which each piece of information is to be expressed must be unambiguously fixed. Words, numbers, or code may be used. In each case, exact meaning must be decided upon and stated. Words have the most flexibility, of course, and codes the least. However, codes are in turn most economical of space. Since the structure of the data file is highly rigid, changes or deletions can be made reaily. Likewise, additions of titles or of categories are conceptually simple and mechanically straightforward. This flexibility of modification is one advantage bought with rigidity of form. This is of great value for any data file that can be expected to change in time.

Another point, perhaps less obvious and surely more controversial is that accuracy of information is of secondary importance while constructing a relationship of inquiry in which data files ultimately work in the personal creation of information. It is not unimportant in the long run, but it is presently less important in the provision of a prototype than are structure and the means to use the file. For this reason, though a diligent attempt was made at accuracy in preparation of the 850 Titles File, no great effort is presently given to its modification and updating. (This is a mechanical task, of less immediate interest than learning to use the file in an imaginative and flexible way.)

Preparation of a large data file of factual information reveals the dependence of such files on large blocks of information prepared for other purposes. The work of agencies such as the Bureau of Employment Security and the Bureau of Labor Statistics is invaluable because many of their results can be taken readily and inexpensively into the file. This suggests three further criteria of data file preparation.

1. Direct preparation of information in large quantities is costly, so that ready-made information sources should be relied upon as far as possible. Some information would eventually have to be gathered and prepared explicitly for the working ISVD, but this must be selected with great care in terms of its cost and and its usefulness.

2. Since ready-made information will seldom exactly suit the purposes it is to serve (unless they are the purposes for which it was explicitly prepared), it must be modified to a form as appropriate to the new use as possible.

3. The need to use as many information sources as possible makes necessary the ability to articulate diverse sources or collections of information into a working whole.

The above three requirements arose directly from the need to make maximum use of available resources. This need might be classed by some as regrettable. It is, however, so universal and unavoidable that it is merely one more fact in preparing information for use by the ISVD. The problem, then, is to handle information in a way that will best serve the uses of the system, given existing technological and economic limitations. In the following pages some steps toward a working solution will be presented.

Clearly the comments here are not limited to information about occupations, though they are derived therefrom and are hence particularly suited to that application. Any data that can be readily described in terms of titles and categories can be treated in this way. Thus these comments have considerable generality. The extent of their applicability must be judged in each individual case, of course.

Further issues of collection and storage of information will be discussed later. First, however, it will be helpful to review some theoretical characteristics of the ISVD as they relate to the preparation of data files.

OF DATA FILES IN THE ISVD

As indicated in the first part of this Chapter "primary data files" had a central role in the operational definition of the ISVD working system. These primary data files are the data files referred to in the present part, of which the file of occupational titles described above is an example. The centrality of these data files within the ISVD thus required their careful articulation with the system as a whole. The considerations that thus arose are of five kinds.

First, the data files (the "primary data files" of the first part) would function in the System together with some form of mediation (the secondary data files and MONITOR of the first part) to help convert the "facts/data" of the files to "information" by individual inquirers in the System. A major task of the System was to provide such mediation. Although the preparation of data files thus does not require the preparation of such mediating elements, the process of mediation will be helped if the data files are properly designed, and if some primitive form of mediation is provided with them. This both justifies and motivates the first steps that were taken toward use of the data files described above. These were:

1. Presentation of the contained information in English language form;

2. Provision for selection of information in terms of certain of its more important characteristics.

These two steps toward conversion of "facts/data" to "information" will be elaborated later.

Second, the process of decision-making by the individual inquirer was conceived in the design of the System as taking place at a number of discrete discontinuities. A central principle of the ISVD was that the inquirer should be helped to maximize awareness of and participation in these discontinuities. The data files in use at any time would be identified in part by the discontinuity the inquirer is dealing with. As the System becomes adept at dealing with a variety of discontinuities, the structure and use of the data files to serve this end must be more and more highly refined. Thus the data files must remain flexible to varying demands depending on which discontinuity is being served. This is further reason why the highly structured form chosen for the occupational data file is appropriate to economical satisfaction of the demands of the System. It permits a single data file to serve a variety of discontinuities.

Third, the theory behind the ISVD prescribed that inquirers be encouraged and taught to deal with their discontinuities in terms of a paradigm of several sequential stages. Again the data files would be called upon to perform differently depending on which of these stages the inquirer is in. Since at any moment each inquirer is likely to be dealing with a different discontinuity and to be at a different stage of the paradigm, great flexibility is demanded of the data files. The structure of data files thus far provided was a step in meeting these needs.

Fourth, the capacity of the inquirer to absorb and use information should have some influence on which information is provided, and how. The same information might be presented in a number of ways, depending on the needs and capabilities of the inquirer. If the data file itself and the means of getting at it are separate (i.e., if more than one means of access and presentation can be adjoined to a single data file) flexibility in use of a single data file would be increased.

Fifth and finally, several means for mediation of "facts/data" to "information" would be used by the System. These include direct teaching of concepts, simulation, and real experience with decision-making. The data files should stand ready to serve these various pedagogical modes. This reinforces the requirements of flexibility, and of access to the files separate and distinct from the files themselves.

YOUNG DATA FILE'S FIRST STEPS

It is clear, then, that the concept of the ISVD and of the operation of data files within it were both highly ambitious. Considerable time was needed to bring them to fruition. There will never be a final system, only a working and evolving system. It is important to distinguish dreams from foreseeable accomplishments, and both from present achievements. The latter are important in that they help to confirm and give hope to the dreams. They also point the way to activities needed to bring foreseeable accomplishment to reality. It is thus desirable to consider application of the 850 Titles File as it has developed, not as a working but never final thing, but as a first step, and as a suggestion of best directions for future development.

It will be recalled that the 850 Titles File consisted of some 850 titles with information in fifty-six categories (prepared for computer use by placing the data for each title on sixteen punched cards; transferred subsequently to magnetic tape). It will also be recalled that this information was almost entirely in compact coded form of little direct use to an inquirer of the ISVD.

An obvious question in converting this data file to use by inquirers was how to present its contents in a form suitable for human comprehension. The answer chosen is fairly simple. As has been noted in Chapter 3, the mechanical problem of presentation of coded information was that of converting it to English or some other readable form. A second problem was that of choosing and interpreting information in a way that is maximally meaningful and minimally misleading. The mechanical problem was simpler, and will be discussed first and more fully.

The form adopted for presentation of information, from the 850 Titles File can be readily described in terms of the mini-data file presented earlier. For each of two occupational titles, this file contained a brief description of the occupation plus certain coded information. During moments of constructing how it can be used somewhat independent of how it will and ought to be used, it is not important whether this information is either appropriate or accurate; it is only important that something be there and be usable as needed. The mini-data file could answer questions such as "What does an egg breaker do?" "How much education does a forest engineer need?" "Where does an egg breaker work?" Answering such questions requires three steps:

1. Identify which category(ies) of stored information contains the answer to the stated question.

2. Find appropriate information by title and category.

3. Present answer in terms understandable to the inquirer.

The first two of the above steps were technical ones, to be taken through accurate identification and location of the stored information. The last could be made by constructing a suitable sentence. An example will suffice. To answer "Where does an egg breaker work?" the System must first identify where information of this type is kept, if it is kept at all. In the illustrative mini-data file, this is the third column of code, in which an "I" or an "O" is found. From this it is possible to respond, "An egg breaker works indoors."

More generally, it can be said: "A (Title) works (x)." This answers the question "Where does a (Title) work?" The System would place "indoors" in the sentence if the data file contains an "I" in the appropriate location, and with "outdoors" if there is an "O." If there are further possible situations such as "both," such a code must be defined, and words provided to interpret that code in the sentence. A special case is the possibility of a blank, or of an illegal answer, in which case some sort of null response would be called for.

The above procedure could be applied with considerable generality, given three things:

1. A skeleton sentence (e.g., "A (Title) works (x).") which makes sense for each possible insertion of (Title) and (x).

2. An English interpretation of the content of the data file for each possible content. This specifies "x" in the above sentence.

3. A substitute message if the coded information is unavailable or inappropriate.

Satisfaction of the above requirements calls for some precision and care, but is by no means impossible or even particularly difficult. Once the rules are set, new titles could be added—or information added, deleted, or changed in the file. Likewise, the form of presentation could be altered without changing the coded information. Thus to a great extent the content and use of the data file could be separated, with resultant valuable flexibility.

It is now a direct step to answering the request, "Tell me about the occupation egg breaker" or, "Tell me about the occupation forest engineer." In either case the answer would be built of the various sentences that answer individual questions about the named occupation. The result will of course seem somewhat mechanical, but with care in preparation it should not be unbearably so. Descriptions for the 850 Titles File have been prepared in this form.

The second question, that of choice and interpretation of information, must be resolved over a longer term, and is much more difficult to handle adequately and honestly. The approach taken so far has been to use whatever data are available, and to be forthright about what they do and do not say. The flexibility designed into the data file and into the presentation of its contents will then facilitate exploitation of improvements in quality of information as they become available.

The structure of the 850 Titles File, its contents, and the presentation of its information in the form described above, have been described in detail in working documents of the ISVD project. Further elaboration of these topics will not be given in this part. The question of access to the information in this file will similarly be treated in a brief manner.

Questions about any individual job readily come to mind, and can be listed more or less briefly, particularly given knowledge of the limited scope of information on each title. The choice of occupation(s) to ask about is far less obvious. To simply present a list of 850 titles and say "You may ask about any of these," would be folly. Such a list in its entirety is of little use. Some method of selective access is needed.

The most direct way of making this choice is in terms of selected characteristics of the titles in the data file. Again we resort to the mini-data file for illustration. The inquirer might ask "Which occupations involve indoor work and require less than a high school education?" The answer would be, "egg breaker." Let us examine this procedure and its limitations.

1. Response to the question can only be in terms of the occupational titles on the list, which is a limitation of the occupational tiles approach. One way of relaxing this limitation will be dealt with presently.

2. Second is the matter of which questions the inquirer can ask the data file. At the present stage of use of the 850 Titles File, questioning is in terms of responses to a set of multiple choice questions. In a fully free situation, one might make other requests, to which the data file could not respond. In that case a "don't know" or "unfortunately an answer on this subject is not available" message would have to be prepared.

3. A third eventuality is exhaustion of the file. With the mini-data file, there are, for example, no outdoor jobs that require less than a high school diploma. With a suitable message, this ceases to be a problem.

Search of the file by the computer for suitable titles is a straightforward matter, subject to the limitations mentioned above.

It is important to remember that the attitude in presentation of data by the System is not prescriptive, but suggestive. Inquirers are not told that they must pursue life as an egg breaker, or even that this is desirable. They are merely informed of this alternative, and that it meets their apparent personal occupational specifications. A description of the occupation, prepared by the System as described above, tells other facts about egg breakers (or forest engineers, or whatever), and gives references to further information. They are then free to try out other sets of specifications, or to accept or reject further consideration of any title, either before or after receiving description of it.

It is important for the inquirer to realize that the System tells what it is asked, and that it can tell no more than it knows. It is the inquirer's responsibility to understand and make use of this fact. If handled properly, a system with incomplete information can be of use to the inquirer. This understanding is imperative, because full information will never be possible. A large and growing body of information could be a reality, however, and can be made responsive to the inquirers' needs, if they know how to deal with it properly.

EXTENSION TO OTHER DATA FILES

Design for an evolving structure of data files within the ISVD can be based on experience with the 850 Titles File. First, however, a final dimension must be added to the problem, namely the possibility of a complex data file composed of two or more files of the type already described.

This extension will be introduced by an example from the actual development of data files for the ISVD. The initial collection of information was made in terms of the 850 Titles File. Information from a variety of sources was coded into a highly structured framework as already described. At subsequent times other information also became available, including:

1. The supplementary volume of the *Dictionary of Occupational Titles* (D.O.T.);

2. Classification by Anne Roe's categories and levels of some 800 occupational titles;

3. Forecasts of demand to 1975[2] by occupation and industry of some 160 occupational groups and some 120 industrial groups.

The availability of this new information posed an important problem in information handling. In each new case the titles covered were substantially different from one another and from those in the originally prepared 850 Titles File. In the case of the supplement to the D.O.T., virtually all jobs of the earlier data file were included, so the additional information could be adjoined readily to the 850 Titles File. Waste arises from the fact that this left more than 90 per cent of the new information unused.

The information about Roe categories and levels (item 2 above) covered about the same number of titles as the original data file. The two lists are far from being equivalent, however. The bulk of the new information could be put to use by

[2] Written in 1967, not 1978

including it where appropriate, and leaving Roe category unspecified elsewhere.

In the case of the forecast information (item 3 above), the situation was considerably different. This information was given not by occupational title but by occupational group. The titles used for groups of occupations and of industries exhaust all possibilities, referring sometimes to titles as "not elsewhere classified." Whereas there exist occupations that are not found in the D.O.T., there are in principle none that do not fall into one of this smaller set of occupational groups. The two classification systems were thus qualitatively different, and must clearly be treated separately.

Information by occupational title and information by occupational group could be articulated by treating one as an example of the other. Thus an example within the group "structural metal workers" is "pneumatic riveter," which is a specific title in the 850 Titles File. Likewise "pneumatic riveter" can be identified as a member of the group "structural metal workers," and through that identification other example titles can be found. Thus the disparity betweeen the two lists could be turned to good use. It adds flexibility to the search for titles of interest.

The above experience can be summarized in general terms as follows:

1. A data file might very well consist of two or more pieces (title-category blocks) that have distinctly different titles and categories of information included in them.

2. Translation between these can be facilitated by suggesting the titles of each block that correspond to each title of the other. These translations need not be unique in either direction.

3. Free use and flexibility of the data files can and should be encouraged by making these translations suggestive rather than prescriptive.

A second case of articulation of the sort described above was carried out between the occupational data file and the military data file. The latter listed categories of assignments for enlisted personnel. This articulation promised to be helpful to the use of both these files.

SPECIFICATIONS FOR THE CONTINUING DEVELOPMENT OF DATA FILES

Data files for the ISVD and procedures for their use were planned to undergo continuing development. There was no foreseeable end to additions or alterations to this material and its uses. Any closed system of data files was to be shunned. A general plan for development was needed in which the data files were continuously operative, but in which new information could be accepted readily and with minimum disruption of operation. Such a plan was suggested by the experience of data file development described above. It derived explicitly from the data files on occupations and military service, but should apply readily to those on education, family living, and other topics an information system like the ISVD might eventually encompass. Needed would be an ability to arrange the information in terms of titles and categories, as mentioned earlier; and to translate among the various sets of titles. The files thus could be readily articulated among themselves. They potentially, therefore, would be not a set of data files, but one large complex file.

Experience so far with data file development suggested certain criteria and a set of rules to meet these criteria. These may seem self-evident or trivial in retrospect, but they were by no means obvious during the development of the data files described here. They might also seem excessively general in form, but this was intentional, to allow application to a wide range of cases.

1. Data files should adapt to different use depending on which discontinuity and stage of decision-making they are serving for each individual inquirer.

2. Means of entry to each data file should be independent

from the file itself, so that either the means of entry or the file itself can be changed without disturbing the other.

3. Likewise, form of presentation of information from a data file should be independent from the file itself for the same reasons.

4. Files should be designed so that additions and updating are possible without undue disruption of the existing files or of their operation.

These criteria, recognized as important in development of the existing data files on occupations and military service, must be interpreted individually for each data file. The following rules were helpful in this regard.

1. Collect information by blocks in which information in well defined categories is given for a set of well defined titles.

2. Entry to these blocks can be according to selected categories, or by title.

3. Coded information should be presented to the inquirer in English or some other readily understandable form. This in general will require structured formats within which to present the information.

4. Free access between separate blocks of information should be facilitated through explicit translation from the titles of one to the titles of the other. Properly done, this will provide flexibility and freedom in finding and taking information from the data files.

Much work remained in the preparation of data files. The job will probably never be over, since updating and additions can be expected to go on so long as there is a System. Three immediate needs, which in 1967 set the stage for the near future, follow.

1. More accurate information, when and as this becomes available in readily usable form.

2. More appropriate information, aimed at individual decision-making rather than economic or large scale planning.

3. Less structured entry to the information. This is mainly a matter of information processing capability and is the task of the System as a whole, not just of the designers of data files.

Section III

STRUCTURING THROUGH PERSONAL PROCEDURALIZATION

A computer literally has many faces. For instance the physical condition of computers varies from computer to computer. However, the physical variation among computers, which is the more common understanding that the computer is not one but many machines, is not actually the more profound of the possible meanings of the statement that the computer has many faces.

The more profound meaning inherent in the statement that the computer is not one but many machines inheres in the fact that *persons* can also individually accomplish variation in any one of several physically different computers. Machines execute procedures. Therefore, the specification of a procedure in effect specifies a machine. A computer program is a specific procedure. Therefore the writing of a computer program is the design of a machine.

Although persons titled computer programmers do in fact write computer programs, not every computer program has to be written by computer programmers. The common man can write computer programs. In fact, very small children can and have written computer programs.

The Information System for Vocational Decisions was based on the presumption that anyone, with instruction, can write computer programs. The system was also based on the understanding that, as Ellis puts it, when you proceduralize something you can computerize it but that to computerize something is not necessarily to proceduralize it. The ISVD made use of this fact in the most basic of its assumptions, namely that *the system is not a system until the person exists in it.* The facts/data in the ISVD are not information until people place themselves in the system and through interaction with it turn the system's facts/data into their information. In order for people to turn facts/data into information they must proceduralize understanding of their information making use of the computerized partial system of public facts/data as well as a partially proceduralized system of processes giving personal meaning to individual intentions as they operate. Proceduralizing understanding of one's information requires the writing of computer programs which can in turn interact with the system's facts/data. Individually written computer programs (i.e., individually constructed machines) therefore become personal servants by means of which each person can process facts/data to comprehend self information.

In the context of the ISVD concept it therefore becomes relevant to address the question, "Can a person and a machine improve understanding of careers?" Since the ISVD "machine" is really the person's proceduralization of personal understanding of personal decision making, the "machine" to which we refer in the ISVD theory is the machine which is the person, or at least that part of which the person is explicitly aware. Therefore for individuals to improve their understanding of their personal "machine" is merely for them to become more articulate about their decisions. The ISVD additionally presumed that increased understanding of decisions maturationally results in eventual comprehension of epigenesis of decision-making development. Epigenesis, or successive differentiation and integration, is a natural part of mentation (Koestler, 1964). Comprehension of epigenesis of decision-making development is a particular potential at least of humans. Comprehension of decision-making development does not necessarily make a person happier or more powerful, merely more aware. The ISVD held that this awareness is good and worthy of cultivation as assiduously as possible, particularly with the assistance of computers since their basic form is the basic form of epigenesis of decision-making development when the person becomes an actual part of their advanced systems.

The above essential understanding of ISVD emerged over the three years in which the principal investigators and staff worked with its resources and requirements. However, Allan Ellis was a principal architect of the understanding on which the above assertions are based. Section I dealt with the assumptions and data of the career process which are at present structured into the ISVD as prototypes in order for the person to grow in comprehension of those processes as specific instances of the more general processes noted above. Section II dealt more specifically with the role of decision-making in information generation, that is, with the computer's understanding of English as a basic theoretical process and with the construction of data files in which information generation through person comprehension of the partial machine understanding of English holds promise of achieving awareness of self responsibility in comprehending epigenesis of decision-making development. This Section remains in the tradition of its predecessors but attempts to enlarge understanding of the fact that we give, *not* pre-empt, responsibility in the ISVD when we computerize some of the career functions without fully proceduralizing them. This is a fact of great consequences to personal motivation.

This Section consists of three chapters. First, Ellis and Tiedeman address the question "Can a machine counsel?" and indicate the basic ISVD form in which the person and the machine are encouraged to improve in their understanding of each other. Next, Tiedeman addresses the question specific to ISVD, namely "Can a machine develop a career?" This Chapter outlines the basic processes of career development which the person will in the ISVD be encouraged to proceduralize with the assistance of the computerized functions of the ISVD. In the last chapter of this section, Tiedeman indicates ways in which the specific career procedure employed in the ISVD can be generalized. "Can a Machine Admit an Applicant to Continuing Education?" deals with generalization from career processes to testing processes, testing processes hopefully more appropriate to the encouragement of self-correcting activity associated with admission processes in continuing education. These admission processes should be considered illustrative of other situations in which personal worth is cooperatively judged such as at work, in marriage, etc.

This Section specifies then the additional explicit steps required to make a theory of guidance in society more explicit.

Chapter 5

CAN A MACHINE COUNSEL?[1]

THE QUESTION AND THE PRIMACY OF PROCEDURE

Just about everyone who spends time trying to figure out what counseling in education is all about agrees that only human beings can counsel. These people—school counselors, professors of guidance, counseling psychologists, and the like—disagree with each other on all the other matters in their profession and this makes the one thing they agree about that much more powerful. Indeed the power of this agreement and the common sense on which it is based make the question, "Can a machine counsel?" a very strange thing to ask. By it we seem to be wondering whether or not something can be human and non-human at the same time, and it must be difficult to imagine how we can take our question seriously. To make matters worse, we are willing to admit, for the duration of the next few paragraphs at least, that people are correct when they say that only human beings can counsel. But we do not consider this any contradiction because we go along with the consensus only to suggest the answer to a question can be unrelated to the posing of it. We assert—and those who recall the works of G. E. Moore, Russell, Wittgenstein, and the other philosophers of language will know this is not a new idea—that the trouble with questions is that they seem so strongly to demand answers. People tend to judge questions by whether or not they can answer them, or on their

[1] This Chapter is based on Project Report No. 17, "Can a Machine Counsel?" by Allan B. Ellis and David V. Tiedeman.

willingness to live with the answers. But questions are good for other things, of course, besides the answers to which they lead.

Our intention with the question is to gain perspective on our feelings about the activity of counseling. One thing a question can do, of course, is lead to other questions, and we hope to get from our perspective a better sense of what those other questions are that must be considered when coming to terms with our idea of counseling. Because of what machines are, we accomplish our task best, we think, by using the word "machine" the way we do in our question.

Machines execute procedures and each machine is the embodiment of the procedure it executes. This is an important relationship that exists for all machines; people are just not in the habit of speaking about machines in this way. It means, of course, that knowing in detail what a particular machine does—how it works—is enough to know what procedure it is executing. The thing that counts about a machine is the way it behaves and this behavior is prescribed by the procedure it executes. All automation, far from being magical as some suppose, is nothing more than the physical expression of well-formed procedures.

When we say that a machine is the embodiment of the procedure it executes, we are saying, in effect, that a statement of a procedure *describes* the machine needed to carry out that procedure. Thus mechanizing means thinking about procedure, not about hardware, and once we state a procedure explicitly we should not really be surprised that a machine can be built to execute it.

To make things simpler in this Chapter we will confine ourselves to computers instead of machines in general. This poses no real restriction, however, since a computer is a device whose job it is to accept descriptions of other machines and to imitate the behavior of those machines. This description is called a computer program and is usually thought of as a set of instructions for what the machine is to do. But a computer program is more like a blueprint which the computer uses to build itself into the particular machine needed to execute the particular procedure described by the program. It is as though the computer were armed with pliers and screwdriver rebuilding itself to conform step-by-step to the elements of our procedure. Having done this the computer becomes the machine our program described, and it will then function as that machine.

A computer without a program will do nothing, whether or not it is plugged in, because computers are not like other machines. In a sense the computer is not a machine at all in its own right, and yet it can become many machines, in fact, any one which can be fully described to it. For example, one may build an address printing machine, or one may write a program which will turn a computer into an address printing machine. In either case the results will be the same with the exception that even though both machines would be operationally equivalent, they would be different from each other in one crucial respect: the computer can do other things tomorrow. Whereas the power of most machines is in what they do, the power of the computer rests in what it can become and the essential idea of a computer is that it is an incomplete machine ready to be completed in an infinite number of ways, each way producing a different machine. Thus a computer program is at the same time an explicit statement of a procedure and the blueprint of a machine needed to carry it out, and whether or not a computer can execute a given procedure depends primarily upon how well we understand the components of that procedure, and how imaginative we are in conceiving procedures in terms of the basic elements of which they are comprised. Centering our attention on a computer, therefore, has the advantage that we depict a machine in terms of such a procedural statement and thus maintain a clearer attitude about machines and their relation to procedures.

Now this attitude about machines is helpful to us because, contrary to first impressions, the form of our question does not impose any preconceived notions on our exploration of counseling. We hope, with this attitude, to avoid the kind of commitment that led Christopher Columbus, for example, to think that Watling Island was the East Indies or the kind of vision that led Abel Tasman to discover two islands in the Southern Hemisphere and at the same time to sail completely around the continent of Australia without ever noticing it was there.

One thing this attitude about machines—and its subsequent application to the activity of counseling—frees us from is a concern about the physical aspects of machines. If there is such a thing as a counseling machine, we need not worry about whether or not it must have arms and legs. Furthermore, we are freed from the somewhat more general worry of whether or not such a machine should be able to smile or frown or nod sympathetically. We may discover later, of course, that these or similar characteristics are necessary parts of our notion of the act of counseling, but our question does not impose this on us and therefore we do not start out needing to believe that such is the case. In this spirit our question represents a point of view about problems. As with all points of view we do not expect resolution from it, but rather some insight into the topography of the problem under consideration. This is why the answer to the question, even if it happens to come out of our analysis, is secondary to the analysis itself.

IMITATION AND MEANING

We begin this analysis by considering the meaning of the question, "Can a machine counsel?" To do this we first look at the procedure adopted by the late Alan M. Turing in his consideration of a similar question. In 1950 Turing, who was an eminent mathematician and logician in England, published an article entitled "Computing Machinery and Intelligence" in which he proposed to examine the question of whether or not a machine can think. His first step was to replace this question by another "which is closely related to it and is expressed in relatively unambiguous words." He said:

The new form of the problem can be described in terms of a game which we call the "imitation game." It is played with three people, a man (A), a woman (B), and an interrogator (C) who may be of either sex. The interrogator stays in a room apart from the other two. The object of the game for the interrogator is to determine which of the other two is the man and which is the woman. He knows them by labels X and Y, and at the end of the game he says either "X is A and Y is B" or "X is B and Y is A." The interrogator is allowed to put questions to A and B thus:

C: Will X please tell me the length of his or her hair? Now suppose X is actually A, then A must answer. It is A's object in the game to try to cause C to make the wrong identification. His answer might therefore be, "My hair is shingled, and the longest strands are about nine inches long."

In order that tones of voice may not help the interrogator the answers should be written, or better still, typewritten. The ideal arrangement is to have a teleprinter communicating between the two rooms. Alternatively the question and answers can be repeated by an intermediary. The object of the game for the third player (B) is to help the interrogator. The best strategy for her is probably to give truthful answers. She can add such things as "I am the woman, don't listen to him!" to her answers, but it will avail nothing as the man can make similar remarks.

We now ask the question, "What will happen when a machine takes the part of A in this game?" Will the interrogator decide wrongly as often when the game is played like this as he does when the game is played between a man and a woman? These questions replace our original, "Can machines think?" (Turing, 1950)

Now, our interest in Turing's approach is in determining if such a procedure for establishing the meaning of the question will work for us. Can we make use of the idea of an imitation game?

Clearly, there are two kinds of imitation possible and even though Turing was never explicit about their differences, it is possible to think about the imitation game in terms of one or the other. The first of these two kinds of imitation we will call Imitation #1 for lack of some better term, although the word "simulation" comes very close to our intended meaning. Imitation #1 consists in the machine *becoming* the thing imitated. Our question, in these terms, becomes, "Can a machine *be* a counselor?" the implication being that the inner workings of the machine would be identical to a counselor, not a particular counselor or even counselors in general. We mean that these inner workings would be such that the resultant behavior would be counseling.

If we replace our question with some test or other, perhaps one like Turing's, that would indicate whether or not a machine is making a successful Imitation #1 of a counselor, we are quickly in trouble. Aside from the formidable difficulties of constructing the test itself, we are faced with the problems posed by all the new questions that arise out of Imitation #1. Because Imitation #1 requires that the machine *become* a counselor, we must expect it to experience all the relevant conditions in which counselors find themselves. If counselors care the machine must care. If they experience the dilemma of the counselee in order to mirror its form and substance, then so must the machine. If it is important that the counselor empathize with the client, then too must the machine empathize, and so on through the range of human conditions essential to counselors when they counsel.

You no doubt see what we get ourselves into by adopting Imitation #1 as our meaning to the question. We are forced to expect the machine to feel what a counselor feels, and this feeling must arise in the same way in the machine as in the human being. But this is a contradiction, making the question nothing more than a word game. To expect something to undergo a human experience is to expect it to become human to that extent. On what grounds, for instance, can we say that a machine that feels and loves and cares is not by that very fact human to some degree? We confuse ourselves with this not because we are led to consider machines to be human even though they are not flesh and blood and do not live and die and breathe, but because our words deceive us into thinking we ask something meaningful, when in fact all we have done is wonder if something that can become human can do human things. In light of these difficulties we reject Imitation #1 as our approach.

The second kind of imitation, which we will call Imitation #2, is essentially the approach adopted by Turing in his imitation game. Imitation #2 consists in the machine *behaving like* the thing imitated and in our case there is some hope in this approach. Our question, in these terms becomes, "Can a machine *behave* the way counselors do?" That is, no matter what the real state of the machine, can it give the appearance of being a counselor?

An imitation counseling game in this case would become a test to see if a machine could do as well as a human counselor in exhibiting all those behaviors which make up the relationship between the client and the counselor. For instance, can the machine *exhibit* concern? Can it seem to be honest and trustworthy? Can it generate confidence? Can the machine make utterances which are relevant and of a kind that assist individuals in dealing with their problems? Compared to Imitation #1, this approach seems much more manageable although we probably do not know enough about the act of counseling to be able to catalogue all the things that must be exhibited by this brand of counseling machine.

We see on closer inspection, however, that Imitation #2 is much more troublesome than Imitation #1 precisely because it seems reasonable. It does not clearly reveal its weaknesses and faulty assumptions and thus can too easily lead us astray. One objection is that Imitation #2 is based on deceit. We believe counselors behave in order to reveal themselves, and this revelation is the mechanism by which they help counselees gain insight. To mirror the counselor's behavior without the substance behind it would be to violate one of our basic premises of what counseling is. Beyond this, Imitation #2 ignores the fact that counseling behavior has its effect only when the client's perception of that behavior is appropriate. Not only must a counselor exhibit honesty, for example; the client must perceive this honesty and believe it. But regardless of its behavior, how do we convince someone that the counselor-machine is honest or concerned or even relevant?

Now these are severe handicaps and yet they are not the worst things about Imitation #2 when applied to counseling. Foremost among the difficulties with Imitation #2 is its assumption that the things human beings do when they counsel are essential to the notion of counseling itself. This is not necessarily the case and we miss the opportunity to consider what is essential when we accept this form of imitation as appropriate. To see what we mean here, consider mountain climbers. In preparing to climb a good-sized mountain, they will, of course, pack a lot of things in their knapsacks including a supply of food. Food is a very important thing on a climb of long duration, but we must be clear about the reason for this. Food is important when you climb a mountain not because it is in any way essential to the notion of mountain climbing, but precisely because human beings climb mountains and human beings must eat at regular intervals. If we build a robot to climb a mountain, no food would be needed.

It may be the same with counseling. Perhaps things like honesty are important in counseling only when human beings counsel. It may be that such things are irrelevant to counseling by machine. Imitation #2 does not allow for this possibility and thus gives up the chance we get by the use of the word "machine" to consider what behavior is or is not essential to our view of counseling. The perspective we gain by our question we would therefore have to give up with Imitation #2. On this ground, as well as on the basis of its other weaknesses, we discard Imitation #2.

Neither kind of imitation will do, it seems, and the expectation that our question can be answered through an imitation game like Turing's must be abandoned. In saying this, we seem to do nothing more than confirm the suspicions the reader must have had at the onset, that the question, "Can a machine counsel?" is a strange and fruitless one to pose. But we do not give up the enterprise because we discard Turing's approach. Indeed, we learn a very important thing from our consideration of the imitation game—a fact which helps us construe our question properly. This is that *all our difficulties with both kinds of imitation stem from the assumption that a machine can counsel only if it can mimic a human counselor.* If we think of our question in a different way—one in which, although we maintain the notion of imitation, we need not expect a machine to ape a counselor—then we can proceed without running such a risk of heresy.

The idea that "imitation" need not mean "copying" is not new. Aristotle, for instance, begins his **Poetics** with a consideration of imitation and Oates and O'Neil tell us, he "is seeking to give a secondary meaning to the term." They say that Aristotle uses the word to mean the process which takes place when an artist creates his work of art. "It is through mimesis (imitation), that form comes to be imposed upon the artist's material broadly conceived," (1938, p. xxiii). That which art imitates is nature, or more accurately, the *process* of nature; and even though the objects of nature are natural and the objects of art are artificial, these objects of art "are produced as nature would have produced them" (McKeon, 1947, p. 621). Art imitates nature in the processes of production as well as in the objects produced.

The difference between art and nature to Aristotle rests in the difference betweeen internal and external causation. He considers nature to be "a cause of motion internal to the thing moved, while art is an external cause employed by the artist to impose on matter a form first conceived in his mind" (McKeon, 1947, p. 621). This distinction is important to our purpose because it is in the play between the internal and the external imposition of form that we can begin to characterize our beliefs about the act of counseling and thus the role, if any, a machine can have in this act.

Artists wish their audiences to undergo an experience and as a result to become more sensitive not to the objects of art themselves but to the natural phenomena which the process of their creation mirrors. Artists differ from others not so much because they can draw or sculpt or write the language well, but because they can experience in a natural phenomenon that which the rest of us can experience only through artistic expression of that phenomenon. Thus, the artistic process—the imitation—is a way of experiencing the world and the object of art is an effort to communicate this experience.

ARTISTRY AND COUNSELING

But this meaning of "imitation" can be used also, we feel, to describe generally the act of counseling, and the mission of the counselor can be thought of as much like that of the artist. The counselors' material is their clients' predicament and the manner in which they establish and develop the relationship between their clients and themselves and their subsequent creation together of the basis for resolution of this predicament constitute the counselors' mode of imitation. The counselors' intent is not merely the resolution of difficulty, but rather the revelation of the *process* by which such resolution becomes possible. They accomplish this through a kind of enactment where form comes to be imposed upon the clients' predicaments first by the counselors' external representation of the process of resolution, but eventually, through insight, by the clients' internal experiencing of the process.

This internalization is the goal the counselor seeks to reach through the essentially artistic activity of revealing, by way of the counseling relationship, the process of resolution. Should the relationship become more important to either of them, then the counselor has failed just as the sculptor fails if his model of Man obscures the experiencing of men from which the sculpting stems.

Now, what all of this means, of course, is that counselors are themselves imitators. When we wonder if a machine can counsel, therefore, we will confuse the issue by expecting the machine to mimic the human counselor because in expecting this we forget that a human being is one kind of medium and a machine is another kind of medium. Because machines and human beings are different media, to expect one to act like the other is much like expecting a poet literally to paint a portrait with words. We must let the machine stay a machine, but recognize that the activity of counseling by human beings is a means to an end, this end being some desired condition in which the client will eventually find himself. Our interest thus centers on the possibilities of a machine achieving this same end even though it does so in a manner clearly different from human beings.

In this way we come to the heart of the question, "Can a machine counsel?" By it we mean to ask: *is it possible to create a machine environment such that an individual who functions in certain specifiable ways within this environment can be said to have been counseled?* We do not ask if a machine can copy what human beings do when they counsel, but rather if we can achieve an identity of goals between a counselor and a machine.

THE GOALS OF COUNSELING

Having settled on this meaning of the question—and thus gained the perspective we need—we are faced with the problem of answering it. To deal with this problem we will first consider what it is a machine must accomplish (notice we do not say what it must *do*) for the answer to our question to be "yes." That is, the primary concern here must be with the *basis* on which the question is to be answered. Following this we can assess the possibilities that such a machine can exist.

Since we pose the question in order to gain perspective on our beliefs about what counseling is, we will at this point present these beliefs although we will be general about it and hardly as explicit as might be desirable. Notice, however, that even though we speak about a particular idea of counseling, the approach to the question is not bound to any specific technique or form of counseling. As a way of viewing the problem, it is general. Thus, we recognize the diversity of opinion that can be tolerated within this approach and we offer one notion of counseling not to argue its merits here but to provide a case in point from which to evolve a basis for an answer to our question.

Counselors, we assert, deal with problems of a particular kind in the manner generally proposed earlier. That is, they deal with these problems by concerning themselves, and hopefully the client, with the processes by which such problems in general may be resolved. In this way some specific problems and the resultant condition in which they leave the counselee are used by the counselor as the material with which to fashion an understanding of the process of problem-solving. This, of course, is the reason why the giving of advice is not enough by itself to amount to counseling.

Now to be more specific about this, we argue that you should send people to a counselor, instead of some other kind of psychologist, when those people have a problem[2] related to their career. The word "career" and the word "problem" are two poor choices of words because in their meanings in ordinary language they do not say all we intend to say. Usually, "career" is used in a far too limited way and "problem" in a far too general way to suit our needs here; but they both, nonetheless, contain the grains of meaning we seek. A brief explanation of our intentions with these two words will clarify the situation.

By "career" we do not mean just a person's job, or occupation, or vocation, or even life's work. These are all parts of

[2] We use the strong word "problem" here even though we consider that a problem is not the only thing that can be an appropriate motivation for seeking counsel. Curiosity, for example, may well be equally appropriate as may be the kind of involvement an individual experiences when in a game-playing mode.

our meaning, of course, but we include much more. In saying that we include more, however, we do not mean to suggest that a career is something that is pieced together or that it is in fact definable by whatever may be included in it, anymore than we would say that the motion of a motion picture is definable in terms of the frames that make up the film or anymore than we would think of electrical current as the piecing together of electrons. Motion and flow are not inherent in the objects that move or the liquids that flow, but rather they are impressions that moving and flowing things leave behind. Thus while motion, for instance, may be implied by objects that move, it is not in the strictest sense made up of those objects.

In this sense career is like motion. We view career—and this is not a very new idea—as the time extended working out of self. This working out of self provides the context and the opportunity for the "expression of hope and desire and limitation upon life" (Tiedeman and O'Hara, 1963, p. iv). By the working out of self, the continuity we call career is created and while purposive behavior is central to the process, we do not consider career strictly as a road that *leads* somewhere. It is, instead, a trace of much the same kind as the bread path of Hansel and Gretel. *Career is the consequence of passage.*

Now the mechanism for this working out of self, and thus for inscription of career, is the activity of deciding and this leads to our meaning of the word "problem." By "problem" we mean some difficulty with deciding. The reason deciding is so important to the process is that it is by the exercise of individual freedom through choice that career becomes the mapping of self instead of just a smoke trail. One difficulty with deciding people might have is the lack of ability to decide: they may not know how to decide. A second difficulty might be that they are not aware of the nature of the decision to be made. Perhaps the most general difficulty people can have—one for which a counselor is most needed—is the inadequate sense that one can decide. At the base of much trouble people have with deciding is the absence of a clear sense that people can be agents in determining what happens in their lives. Later, we will say more of this sense of agency and its relation to the development of self.

The specifics of the process of decision-making may be characterized by way of a paradigm proposed in 1963 by Tiedeman and O'Hara. In confining the paradigm to the rational form of decision-making they state: "It seems sufficient to suggest a paradigm of the process of reaching a rational decision since such is the differentiated and later integrated condition that the practices of guidance attempt to facilitate." (p.38) It is through the notion of decision-making as depicted in this paradigm that we will view the counselor's effort to impose form on the client's predicament and thus to reveal the processes by which the imposition of such form can be generally achieved.

According to the paradigm, the process of decision-making is divided first into two aspects called *anticipation* and *accommodation*. The anticipation aspect consists essentially of a person's preoccupation with the pieces—facts, alternatives, options, consequences—out of which a decision is to be fashioned and with the aspirations, hopes, expectations, constraints, and the like which will determine the form of the decision. The accomodation aspect—also called "the aspect of implementation or adjustment"—represents the movement from anticipation to induction; it is the point where imagination meets reality. In the case of both anticipation and accommodation it is possible to speak about "subaspects" or stages.

The first stage of anticipation, called exploration, begins with a person's awareness "that a problem does or will exist and a decision must be reached in order to resolve it in a satisfying manner." (p. 38) In discussing exploration, Tiedeman and O'Hara state:

> In the step of exploration . . . a number of different alternatives or possible goals . . . may be considered. Relevant goals are those which can possibly be attained from the opportunities associated with the problem under considera-

102   VALUE DEVELOPMENT

tion. . . . During the exploratory step fields are relatively transitory, highly imaginary (perhaps even fantastic), and not necessarily related one to the other. They may be a relatively unassociated set of possibilities and consequences. . . . In the step of exploration in relation to a problem of career development, a person probably reflects at least upon his aspiration, opportunity both now and in the future, interest, capability, distasteful requirements that still can be tolerated, and societal context for himself and his dependents. These are relevant aspects of the field set by each goal. In short, a person attempts to take the measure of himself in relation to each alternative as he senses it. (pp. 28 and 41)

Of *crystallization*, the second stage of anticipation, they assert:

In (crystallization) the cost of the several goals can be considered in relation to the return from each. The value of alternatives can then be assessed. Relevant considerations are organized or ordered in this process of valuing. . . The process of valuing gives rise to values which tend to fix the organization or order of all relevant considerations in relation to each of the goals as crystallization occurs. . . . . Crystallization normally represents a stabilization of thought. A setting of thought is achieved which is ordinarily of some durability and hence of some reliance. This set readies the person for investment of self along a line that then becomes more noticeable. The situation becomes defined, so to speak, at least for a time. (p. 41)

The third stage is that of choice and it follows readily on the heels of crystallization. Quoting again from Tiedeman and O'Hara:

With *choice*, a particular goal, and its relevant field . . . orients the behavioral system of the person of relevance for his problem. . . . This goal may be elected with varying degrees of certainty and its motive power will vary as a result. . . . Furthermore, the degrees of clarity, complexity, and freedom generally available to the person in the solution of this problem and in the pursuit of the indicated decision will also affect the motivating power of the resulting resolution of alternatives. (p. 42)

The fourth and final stage of anticipation is called *clarification*. You would expect that once a choice had been made that aspects of decision-making which precede action would have been finished. But even though the decision is made and held firmly, often doubt about the decision will arise. This is true.

. . . in even a short period of waiting (a week or more, say) for the expected situation to begin to unfold . . . doubt experienced in the waiting period causes the individual further to clarify his anticipated position. An elaboration and perfection of the image of the future . . . ensues. . . . *Clarification* not only perfects the image of self in position, but also dissipates some of the former doubts concerning the decision. (p. 43)

The three stages of accommodation may be briefly described in the following way:

Induction: . . . A general defense of self and a giving up of an aspect of self to group purpose; . . . the individual's goal and field assimilatively become a part of the region . . . of the social system in which the person is implementing his desired solution of his problem. He learns the premises and structures-in-interaction required for continued identification. This process leads to a further perfection of individual goal and field in social system. . . .

Reformation: . . . The receptive orientation of induction (*gives*) . . . way to (*an*) assertive orientation. . . . The person is well immersed in a relevant group. . . . He has a strong sense of self and actively enjoins the group to do better. . . Since . . . the person acts both upon the in-group and field . . . in order to bring that group into greater conformance with his modified goal and field . . . and upon the out-group to bring their view of his identification into greater consistency with his, the effect, if any, is the modification of group goal and field . . .

Integration: Synthesis is, of course, the essence of integration. . . A differentiation in identification has been achieved. The new-found appreciation of self is integrated with its larger field. This new part of the self-system becomes a working member of the whole self-system. In integration, individual and group both strive to keep the resulting organization of collaborative activity. . . . The individual is satisfied, at least temporarily, when integration occurs. (p. 44)

Now there is something peculiar about this paradigm; a potential difficulty quite similar to the problems we sometimes get into when we use language. A peculiarity of language known to philosophers for some time is that among the things we use language to talk about is language itself. Bertrand Russell, for example, has shown that it is a case of bad "philosophical syntax" to assert something like, "The golden mountain does not exist," and from this suppose you are attrubuting some kind of existence to the very thing whose existence is denied in the sentence. As language does sometimes, the paradigm of decision-making turns back onto itself in a way we must be clear about. Not only does the paradigm depict the decision process, it also by this depiction, prescribes how one should relate to that process. That is in enunciating the aspect of accommodation, the paradigm argues that one of the things to which one must accommodate is the decision process itself. But integration is the development of meaning that is independent of language as the instrument of that meaning. Thus, the language of decision-making, even though it is the medium through which understanding of the process comes, must be thrown off before the accommodation is complete.

This throwing off—perhaps making invisible is a better thing to say—of the instrument of meaning gets us back to the play between the external and the internal imposition of form we spoke of earlier. Accommodation to decision-making itself is the most general kind since it represents internalization of the *processes* of resolutlion. First the language must be established for the individual (induction), then it must itself become an object of analysis (reformation), and finally it must dissolve, as the individual goes past it to meaning (integration).

By way of the essentially artistic activity described earlier, counselors must take their clients through these phases, not with respect to a particular problem so much as with respect to the process itself. They must establish the clients' proficiency in the language of the process, develop their awareness of this language and its effects, and, in the end, facilitate each individual's internalization of this process. In doing this, we argue that the counselor leaves the client with a sense of agency as a logical consequence. The state in which one believes oneself to be a significant agent in determining what happens to one comes not from convincing one about it but from the internalization of the decision process.

RECONSIDERATION OF THE QUESTION

Having said all of this—briefly and with hardly enough explanation—about our views of counseling we can now pursue the terms under which an answer to the question we pose in this chapter might reasonably be formulated. In the most general sense, before we would be willing to say that a person has been counseled by machine, this machine would have to accomplish at least three things. First it would have to reflect the elements of decision-making in such a way that the lantuage of the process was exposed to the client. Naturally this exposure of the language must lead to the development of the individual's proficiency in its use. Second, the machine must encourage the development of awareness of the process and the relation of self to problems as viewed by that process. That is, the process must become a mechanism for the manipulation of this relationship between self and predicament. Finally, the machine must allow and foster the individual's accommodation to the decision process both in terms of specific predicament and, more important, in terms of the process in general. Remember, because we seek *identity of goals* between machine and counselor we need not expect this act of counseling to be carried out the same way by each.

But this is easy enough to say and, even though the idea of identity of goals enhances our perspective and subsequent analysis, we have no reason yet to suppose that a machine can accomplish anything resembling what we need. To repeat the point we made in the first paragraph, however, we really do not have to bother with what it would take specifically for a machine to counsel. What we are hoping for with this argument is that readers will be encouraged to ask our question about their view of counseling. In our case we should go back and examine the many roads we have opened for ourselves. We should wonder, for instance, what a human counselor can do to achieve the ends of counseling as they have emerged from our attempt at the question. Are certain techniques more defensible than others? Are the honesty or the concern or the objectivity of a counselor important techniques or essential conditions of counseling? Are there pedagogical issues central to the achievement of the goals of counseling?

Even though such questions must be dealt with carefully and fully before we will know enough to talk in any but a superficial way about machines and counseling we will nonetheless attempt an answer here. For two other reasons, the answer will be bad. First, it will be an answer by example which is the coward's way out. Second, it is a weak example. But some of our previous argument will at least be clarified by this attempt at an answer.

There is an old oriental saying that if a man has one hundred miles to walk, he is wise to consider himself half way there only when he has walked ninety miles of the journey. By such reckoning our example is hardly more than a glance in the direction we wish to go. For our example we describe the ISVD project as it existed after only about two years of work on it.

As has been noted earlier, the theory underlying the ISVD project deliberately plays upon a potentially useful distinction between *data* (facts) and *information* (facts interpreted in relation to use). The task of the information system is to enable individuals to transform data into information. This is to be done by teaching them to interpret the data in the light of their own knowledge, experience, and intention, so that their organization and use of the data represents their own personal relationship to the data in the process of decision-making. We presume that only when data are used in this way can they be described as information where individuals are concerned. The information so generated can then, in turn, serve as data in the making of future decisions. Given that the quality of decisions is directly related to the kind, quality, and comprehensiveness of the *information* (i.e., data in relation to personal intention) considered by the individual during the process of decision-making, then a fundamental task of guidance is to identify, evaluate, and classify needed data *and to make them readily available to inquirers in usable forms and at needed times and places.*

Throughout individuals' passage from point to point in the decision-making process, they continue to engage in the act of turning data into information. This is a major concern of the project, since, in the real world, data are never complete and neither is information. Often, it is precisely this incompleteness that makes decisions necessary in the first place. In any event, the quality of the choice depends upon the quality of the data. Before one attempts to make a decision, therefore, one must first understand the incompleteness of the data and information with which one is dealing.

Accepting data and information on these terms leads naturally to the condition that one is more likely to take responsibility for the choices one makes, since they are not totally determined by external factors. If they were, then choice would be either irrelevant or superfluous. Furthermore, in order to create information on which to base decision, one must actively process data rather than passively be guided by them, and therefore, individuals must become significant agents in the choice process. That is, the incompleteness of data implies that individuals are *responsible* for their decisions in both meanings of the word: they are the ones who make the decisions, not someone or something external to them; they are the ones who enjoy or suffer the consequences. This is one way to define "freedom" and it is to this notion that the project is dedicated. It will achieve this goal by developing in the inquirer the ability to engage in this kind of decision-making relative to career choice. That is, the project would place inquirers among resources, enhance their access to them, teach them the stages in decision-making, and have them engage the resources in a controlled setting so that they can develop the skills of processing data and making decisions.

An additional factor in the decision-making procedure which this project proposed is called *monitoring* and consisted in keeping track of the inquirers as they go from stage to stage through the paradigm time and again. Aside from the usual reasons for monitoring inquirers' behavior—to anayze their performance, select from alternate courses of action, and generally maintain an account of their interaction with a system—the project expected to present to them the facts of this monitoring so that they might use them as additional data. These facts become a kind of meta-data which the inquirers process. The idea of data and meta-data is analogous to the philosophical notion of being and becoming. Not only do individuals act but they become aware of their pattern of action. The desired result is a higher order of understanding of both the decision-making act and the panorama of career choice in which decision points are linked. Career becomes a time-extended set of choices, and decision at any given point is enhanced by an overall awareness of the road being travelled.

What the project proposed, then, is a model of decision-making behavior which requires a setting capable of providing feedback and of generating feedforward, the individuals' feedforward, that is. It is an interactive setting in which individuals engage one or more data files in certain specifiable ways as a means of determining alternatives and of selecting from among them on bases understood to themselves.

The setting we sought is one which will develop in inquirers the ability to engage in the decision process as depicted by the paradigm described earlier. Some of us called this setting a reckoning environment because we wanted inquirers to do more than just make up their minds. We wanted them to figure up, measure, estimate, compare, judge, make calculated guesses, and in the end decide *and* take responsibility for their decisions. This, of course, is what "deciding" means, but often people equate decision-making with choice-making and thereby miss the inherent notion of the process and its extension over time. What is left, usually, is the mistaken idea that people decide by making up their minds, and thus we hear about the moment of decision as though it all happens at a point in time which is discrete and unbounded by thought and reflection. To make it clear that it is precisely this misconception and the resulting inflexibility we wished to challenge in ISVD, we have come to refer to *the setting for vocational decision-making which we are creating as a vocational reckoning environment.*

Once we recognize the obvious fact that data and information are never complete it becomes wise—often vital—to place the condition on choice that it be made with the best possible data available. We must ask of the data: Are they *accurate?* How *complete* are they? Do they reflect the full *complexity* with which we must deal? Can we get them in *time* to explore alternatives adequately? A library is unsatisfactory in this area, because the time involved in searching is often more than the individual can afford. Certainly large amounts of data—occupational descriptions, for example—can be stored, indexed, cross-referenced, and made generally available in a library, but that is only part of what is needed. The computer, on the other hand, is capable of all this and of providing fast access so that search time need not hamper decision-making. Furthermore, the computer can interact with inquirers and thereby help them to ask relevant questions about the world of work. The project looks to the computer, therefore, as a device to store large amounts of occupational data and to make them immediately and selectively available to individuals as they proceed through the decision-making process. With this kind of accessibility, individuals can feel they are among resources and as they become more integrated into the reckoning environment, the data becomes more like extensions of them and less like external qualities, that is, the data move toward becoming information.

Along with the inquirers themselves there were planned two additional components within the ISVD reckoning environment. The first of these was an extensive collection of data about the world of work, military service, and education. Facts about jobs, colleges, trade schools, military specialties, and about inquirers themselves are just a few of the types of data to be stored and made available to them. These data were organized into five major data files: occupational, military, educational, personal and family living, and student characteristics. Naturally, while each of these files was separate from the other, they all referenced each other so that an inquirer might follow a question through all its aspects.

Between the inquirer and the data we intended to place a guidance machine. The function of this third and final element of the ISVD reckoning environment was to facilitate inquirers' access to data and vice versa. That is, not only did we wish to provide a means for the inquirer to gain convenient access to data, but we wished to keep track of such access as well. In this way, not only could individuals get facts with which to make decisions, but they could also gain a sense of the way they go about making decisions.

One way to describe the ISVD reckoning environment is shown in this diagram.

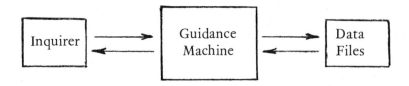

We in ISVD called our machine a guidance machine and we will use this term for the rest of this chapter even though our intention here is to suggest that its behavior approaches counseling.

Now, it was the purpose of ISVD to create a sufficiently explicit description of the behavior of a guidance machine so that a computer can behave as though it were that machine. Our efforts to create a description of a guidance machine fell into two categories. The first was the development of "Necessary Software." This consisted of a fairly elaborate set of computer programs which permitted certain basic and generally required functions to be performed. We needed, for example, to operate in a time-shared setting so that more than one individual can use the system at any one time. Furthermore, we had to provide the ability to create, maintain, edit, and retrieve data files. A programming language to allow both string manipulation and list processing, programs for statistical analyses, routines to permit content analysis, and the general facility of keeping track of who is on the system and what needs to be done next are some other examples of the kind of Necessary Computer Software with which we had to be concerned.

The second category, and perhaps the most interesting one, was the development of ISVD software. These were the programs that enabled our time-shared computer to behave like a guidance machine, and it is here that any substantive contributions of ISVD rest.

The chart on the following page depicts in a general and incomplete way the overall organization of the ISVD software.

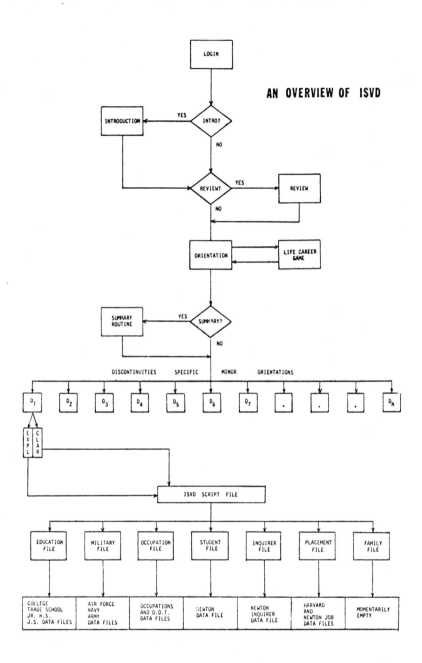

AN OVERVIEW OF ISVD

DESIGNING OUR CAREER MACHINES 113

This software may be divided into four parts each of which plays a role in the inquirer's development of a sense for the decision process.

The first of these parts consists of the ISVD data files. In the chart these data are represented in the last two lines. Thirteen such data files are included thus far, and our plan is to let this number increase as need for new files arises.

Even though the thirteen data files that were originally going into ISVD were different from each other in a number of respects, they were essentially alike in overall structure. A brief description of one of the data files, therefore, will provide an indication of what the rest were like. The one we will describe is the occupations data file.

The occupations data file contains about fifty facts on each of about eight hundred and fifty occupations. These facts relate to such things as wages, education, physical demands, worker traits, high school courses needed, and the like. The fifty or so facts about each occupation are grouped together to form a record. We call these level-zero records and, of course, there is one level-zero record for each occupation.

In addition to these records, we made provision for including hierarchical records—level-one, level-two, and so forth—which may be thought of as summary records. The level-one records in the occupations data file, for instance, are used to represent simultaneously many different *logical* organizations of the data without concern for their *physical* organization. One set of such records might be used to characterize the records in terms of the Roe categories while another set might represent someone else's taxonomy.

Besides these two kinds of records, the occupations data file contains a fairly extensive collection of incomplete, but completable, English sentences of the form. "The salary of X is Y," or "To be an X requires Y years of education." If an inquirer should ask something like, "How much do doctors earn?" or "How long do I have to go to school to become a plumber?" then the variables X and Y in these template sentences would be replaced by the appropriate facts and presented. The use of these template sentences—and paragraphs—need not be as trivial as the example offered here.

The version of ISVD described here—called Prototype I—contains in its thirteen data files several million data potentially relevant to career choice. This part of the ISVD software, while in no sense complete, was nonetheless sufficiently extensive to allow non-trivial exploration.

As extensive as these data are, however, the single, most significant component of ISVD software is that network of routines we called *scripts.* Not unlike the manuscript of a play (from which it was given its name) a script is a set of rules describing how the guidance machine is to act. Scripts contain such things as the text to be presented to an inquirer via either a video display device or a printer, commands to activate a tape recorder, or motion picture projector, or to display a 35mm slide, instructions for how to process the individual's responses, and rules for any computation or storage or retrieval of data.

Some scripts deal with the concepts underlying the decision process and are called teaching scripts. These scripts superficially resemble the usual computer-aided-instruction material. Preference scripts are a second kind. They are used to assist inquirers in their consideration of the factors on which choice may be based. The taking of a preference script has the effect of processing the associated data file, leaving behind only those records that conform to the stated preferences. Finally, direct access scripts are used to retrieve specific bits of data from the files.

A third part of the ISVD software was called the Access Routine. EXPLORATION, CLARIFICATION, and REVIEW Access Routines served to engage the inquirer in behavior representative of the decision paradigm. They are used like filters between the inquirers and their access to data and in this way are supposed to develop their proficiency and their awareness of the decision process. In Access Routines must rest the artistry which is inherently that of counseling. An example of the Access Routine in action was given in Chapter 3.

The fourth part of the ISVD software consisted of those routines that form the backdrop of the system. These elements perform the task of getting individuals to the appropriate place in the system. When inquirers "log on" the system they are given an introduction should they need one. They are then asked what they wish to do. The backdrop routines process their answers and determine which discontinuity (in the chart, D_1, D_2 etc.) they are dealing with. Another routine then determines whether they are in exploration or clarification with respect to this discontinuity and pass them through the appropriate access routine. From there they will be provided access to the relevant scripts for their situations and these scripts will in turn provide the needed access to the data bases.

This description is an oversimplification, obviously, but it makes the point of how we intended the guidance machine to function. That is, it indicates in a general way how we hoped to develop—through scripts—the inquirer's proficiency with the elements of decision-making and—through access routines—the inquirer's awareness of the process underlying these elements. These are two of the three things which we earlier asserted a machine or a human being must accomplish to be said to be counseling.

The third requirement we listed was that the machine must allow and foster the individual's accommodation to the decision process. This, of course, is the heart of the matter.

In our development of the first prototype of ISVD we dealt with this third requirement least of all. It was clearly the most difficult issue we faced, and although we had certain hunches about it, we were not yet as clear as we would like to be. One hunch concerned the monitoring function, and we have already described how we used the monitoring of individual interaction with the system as a means to reveal the process and the individual's relation to it.

Another hunch concerns the Life Career Game and other games we planned for the system. The Life Career Game developed by Sarane Boocock (1967) and others allows a person

to develop and go through a life plan for any number of ficti-
tious people. By using this game we hoped to have the inquirer experience some of the more realistic concomitants of
choice. We placed the game where we did in the chart to indicate that it is not merely a component of the ISVD system.
We thought of it as a point of view about the system in general. That is, inquirers could use the ISVD either for real
(with their own interests) or as someone they pretend to be.
The two major gains with the game are the objectivity one
has by dealing with someone else's predicaments, and the extension over as much as twenty (simulated) years that the
game provides. As strong as these hunches were, however, we
did not have enough experience to tell much about them.

One small force for accommodation to the system and
thus to the decision process it reflects is the ISVD command
language. With this simple language inquirers could take over
control of the system flow moving about in the system the
way they wished.. This is very much the kind of behavior
characteristic of the integration stage of accommodation and
in this way we see the *possibility* that one can indeed accommodate to a machine based system and thus to the process
embodied by the system. We recognize that this is somewhat
of an overstatement, and we would be more careful about it
if our intention was to argue that ISVD's guidance machine
can indeed counsel. We have no such intention.

We described ISVD to provide a sense of what ISVD could
eventually become rather than of what it was when the USOE
contract expired. Relating to the question of this sub-section,
ISVD is not a case in point because it can prove or disprove
anything about this question. On the contrary, in this case
ISVD would be irrelevant. We describe ISVD to show a little
bit of the relationship that exists between a process and its
mechanization. It is here that ISVD is significant.

It is, of course, common sense to say that something must
be proceduralized before it can be mechanized and the signi-
ficance of ISVD is that it clarifies what this means. That is,
when thinking about whether or not a machine can counsel,

do not be deceived into assuming that the thing that must be proceduralized is the *act* of counseling. If you assume this you inherit all the difficulties of Imitation #1 and #2 . But if you wonder, instead, what an environment might be like which has the effects of counseling in terms of what one who functions in this setting is thereby encouraged to become, then even if you decide no machine could ever be a part of this environment, you will have been left with a clearer notion of what your concept of counseling demands.

Now everything we have said in our attempt to answer the question, we recognize, is weak on at least two counts. First, of course, our assertions and our analysis of them need much more consideration if they are to become in any sense firm and sturdy. Second, not only is our example a long way from ideal, there may be no ideal to be reached. In constructing ISVD we went far enough to know for sure we could go further. The contract was not renewed to make further advances possible.

These are important limitations, but even though we have taken the question seriously enough to attempt an answer, our intention is to offer in the question a fresh look at some assumptions about counseling that are rarely challenged. We expect quarrels over our answer because we know it is simple-minded and a bare first attempt. We hope, however, that these quarrels will not discourage you from seeing in our strategy an opportunity to start from scratch with the problem of what counseling is all about and of how machines may enter into the procedures of counseling when the goals of counseling and for the machine are consonant.

Chapter 6

CAN A MACHINE DEVELOP A CAREER?
PROCESSES OF EXPLORATION AND COMMITMENT IN CAREER DEVELOPMENT[1]

PROCEDURALIZATION AND CAREER

As indicated earlier, ISVD was conceived so as to facilitate comprehension of epigenesis as successive differentiation and integration in decision-making development associated with career evolution. The previous chapter used the general ISVD notion that something can be computerized without fully proceduralizing it beforehand to indicate how a machine can provide a counseling environment. We also there illustrated how opportunity for repeated choice-making about education, occupation, and military service could be arranged in ISVD to let a person induce the structure of decision-making procedure which must personally be introduced into the computerized environment of choice-making if the supposed "machine" of decision-making is to be internalized in the ISVD counseling environment.

The intent of ISVD was to proceduralize choice-making in order to facilitate an inquirer's gradual generalization of choice-making to an understanding of decision-making both specifically and generally. "Career" is the primary concept in that generalization. Computerization of the concept of career

[1]This chapter is based on Project Report No. 16A, "Can a Machine Develop a Career? A Statement about the Processes of Exploration and Commitment in Career Development" by David V. Tiedeman.

which makes possible the transfer of its proceduralization from the computing environment to the person requires specification of the career concept which is to be computerized and internalized through the person's proceduralization of it in the ISVD counseling environment. We outline that specification in this chapter.

We again address specification of the concept of career through examination of the general question, "Can a Machine X?" However, since the specific question we address in this chapter is "Can a machine develop a career?" we employ a strategy different from that used in the previous chapter. Where in the previous chapter we avoided effort to specify a procedure which the machine would imitate, in this chapter we first lay out a procedure which the machine could be programmed to imitate. We do so because the X of our general question is in this chapter *both* the act of development and the object of career where the X in the prior chapter was *only* the procedure of counseling. Therefore the task of this chapter is to lay out the meaning of development and career. However, we do so in ways by which attainment of those understandings by persons will still remain consistent with the environment of counseling specified in the prior chapter.

AN IMITATION CAREER
AS INSTRUMENT IN CAREER DEVELOPMENT

A Time Chronology

A machine is programmed to record the dates on which individuals enter and leave each event in their work history. If this record was feathered out so that it also gave the hours of particular days on which the people worked as well as their dates, the chronology would more accurately portray the position which the individuals gave work in the time use pattern of their lives. However, such a record would become more complicated than it has so far been made in vocational psychology. Therefore, we conceive the chronology in its presently limited sense.

The dates which people worked at each of the several jobs held when related to their advancing age portray aspects of work in which we have only recently become interested, namely the length of time people stay on a particular job. Presumably, the length of time people stay on a particular job increases as they grow older. However, technological change is having considerable effect on this fact at the present time. Technological change is also having effect on the number of jobs which people are likely in the future to record in their chronology.

A Work Vita

If we programmed the machine to record the names of the jobs an individual held in each of the periods worked as well as the company in which the job was discharged, other matters in vocational psychology spring into being. We think of jobs in terms of their kinds, their responsibilities, and of the companies in which they are practiced. When we think of jobs in terms of their kinds we frequently call those kinds, "occupations." We thus consider occupation to be a more general term than a job. By making reference to the job and enterprise codes of the *Dictionary of Occupational Titles* (1966) stored in its memory, our machine could indicate the occupations at which an individual has worked. Our machine memory could also contain the occupational level codes of Holland (1966) and/or Roe (1956). The machine could therefore write a work vita which incorporates inferences about the level of responsibilities an individual has held and now holds. The memory of the machine could also include Super's (1957) code of enterprise. The program could therefore incorporate in the work vita inferential data about the kinds of work organizations in which the work has been and is performed.

The memory of the machine could also include Roe's (1956) group categorization of occupations. A program could be written based on these group classifications which infer the vocation which a person is pursuing. This program could be based on the consistency of the groups in which people's occupations fall as they change work. The program for inferring occupation would also compare the levels of an individual's several jobs as well as their groups. A vocation associated with progress in advancement level would be called a career. Persistent advances in level accompanied by changes in groups and/or enterprises would be referred to a new table which would contain career names different from vocation names based on Roe groups. Records of uniform level with the variability in Roe groups would be referred to still another career table to find names appropriate for such records. Records with vacillating levels and groups would be referred to still another type of career table to name the career. Finally, career names associated with employment in the same group at vacillating levels would be obtained from still another type of career table. The machine could also contain a table permitting the inference of interests from the work organizations in which an individual has been employed. This table would particularly differentiate self from company types of employment and in the latter case differentiate work style based on inference about work groups. Inferences about vocation, career, and work style would be further referred to tables from which personality characteristics would be inferred.

Personality Organization[2] in the Work Chronology and Vita

An individual's naming of the job and the company in

[2]Tiedeman is primarity indebted to Gordon Dudley and Eileen Morley for teaching him about the terms and concepts of organization as used herein.

which it is practiced could also be referred to the stored *Dictionary of Occupational Titles* for reference to description of its duties and prerogatives, the interpersonal, material, and ideational relationships it requires and permits, and the experiencing style it requires and permits in relation to the experiencing style effected in the non-work environment. Suppose that we consider as structure the three elements in each kind of description, namely, 1) requirements and prerogatives, 2) interpersonal, material, and ideational relationships required and permitted, and 3) the experiencing style required and permitted. Furthermore, let us consider the function of aspiration in growth or effective curiosity as we might better conceive growth. Then we can consider as organization in personality the change from one structure to another which one attempts and effects as one vocationally responds to aspiration in growth. Although we cannot specify the detail at the moment, let us suppose that we can write programs which infer organization when structures are compared, pair by pair in sequence.

When the vocational history has been programmed sufficiently for organization to exist, it becomes possible to conceive development. What develops in vocation is the organization of occupational structures in service of the aspiration function. What develops in our program of vocational development is the linguistic context within which we explain the vocational aspects of the life history.

Education
and Work Chronology and Vita

Suppose that the machine could be further programmed to record an educational chronology and vita as well as the work chronology and vita. When the work history is joined with an educational chronology and accompanying naming of the educational experiences associated with each of several discrete periods, we must recognize that education is no longer necessarily all concentrated before work. Therefore, two relationships of interest in vocational psychology must be programmed. One relationship which must be programmed is the *interspersing* of education and work. The other relationship which must be programmed is the *interdependence* of education and work. At the present time this interdependence can be either *preparatory* as it has traditionally been or *synergetic* as it may well more frequently become. In the synergetic condition we might well conceive a job as causing us to know that we must personally expand knowledge from education and to act upon what knowledge we have and that prior fact while continuing in jobs.

Some of the aspects of the named educational experience which must be programmed because of their interest in vocational psychology are those associated with 1) the kind of school a person is in during a period, elementary, secondary, tertiary, for instance, and 2) the subjects studied. The kinds of schools attended must be programmed to relate with the conception of level in occupation. The Cooley and Lohnes (1968) career tree will be helpful in the preparation of this program. However, in broader outline, the subjects a person pursues could be programmed to bear both on level in one sense but on kind of occupation in a more important sense. It is the relationship of subject and occupation in the *preparatory* relationship of education which gives rise to entry into an occupation. It is the relationship of subject and occupation in the *synergetic* relationship of education which gives rise to satisfaction, success, and possibly progress in career.

Personality Organization in the Education and Work Chronologies and Vitae

Suppose that we can do for education what we have suggested can be done for occupation, namely to expand by way of some dictionary or school catalogue an individual's naming of the schools and subjects in the individual educational history. We could then program into our machine the provision of the requirements and prerogatives, the interpersonal, material, and ideational relationships required and permitted, and the experiencing style required and permitted for each school and subject. If we then again consider organization in personality to be the change in one structure to another which people attempt and effect as they respond vocationally to aspiration in growth, we can again imagine a machine program written so that various characteristics of the personal educational organization may be inferred from comparison of these structures in sequenced pairs. The details of this machine program still remain as necessary tasks to be undertaken, not as completed studies. We do not know much about how epistemological understanding grows.

The existence of educational as well as occupational organization introduces another problem in career which our machine program must handle. Tiedeman has previously noted the essentially preparatory and synergetic relationships which education may have with occupation in the career. We note here that this relationship may in addition vacillate from time to time in the career. Therefore, our programs which write the interrelationship of education and occupation from chronologies and vitae in those dual realms must pay particular attention to the relationship which one organization is from time to time given opportunity to have on its conterpart organization.

Gribbons' conception of vocational readiness planning (Gribbons and Lohnes, 1968) could provide one of the frameworks for programming the intersection of educational and occupational realms in the career. Crites' (1965) and Super's conceptions of vocational maturity (Super and Overstreet, 1960), could also provide a still higher order conception for programming of that intersection. Finally, Super's metadimensions of self concept (cf. Super, Starishevsky, Matlin, and Jordaan, 1963) as expanded by O'Mahoney's (1968) theory of vocational self concept could provide the programming guides for the intersection of vocation and career.

Personality Organization
in Expanded Chronologies and Vitae

The imitation career has so far been described first in terms of a chronology, next in terms of a vita, and finally in terms of a personality organization of each of two realms of activity, educational and vocational. As these descriptions were undertaken, we also noted that the issues in machine programming involved the existence of a dictionary from which structure can be inferred in each realm. Organization can then in turn be inferred by conceiving the problem of expanded linguistic meaning which arises from sequentially juxtaposing the structures of pairs in a single realm presuming that structure is changing in service of the function of growth. Finally, we noted that the existence of two organizations added to the problem of inference that of causing the organization in one realm to be programmed in interaction with the organization in the other. In the interaction we proposed that a critical factor should be the programming of the dominating or coordinating effect of one structure on another as organization changed in the function of growth. In this regard, Super's theory of vocational development (1957) might serve as a first order approximation of the needed programming. However, in all likelihood we will need many more studies on the order of that of O'Hara (1958) which dealt developmentally with the dominating and coordinating effects of awareness in several realms of vocational self concept over each of several years.

The programming so far described can therefore first be considered as a general description. Chronoligies, vitae, and organizations in additional realms could then also be programmed to the extent that dictionaries of structure and developmental theories of organization are available. The addition of each new realm must of course be programmed so that its effects will be written independently of other effects, in pair-wise interactions with each other effect, in triad-wise interactions of all effects, and so on up to the final single interaction equal to the total number of realms included in the momentary definition of career in personality.

Matthews (1960) demonstrates that personal and family living is an effect of great importance to career in personality. The programs in the imitation career must therefore also include the structures of marriage and family. It is not yet very possible to write machine programs for the development in personality which includes marriage and family structures. However, Friend and Matthews have case material from which fair approximations will be possible, at least for women. Furthermore, Super's Career Pattern Study (Super, Crites, Hummel, Moser, Overstreet, and Warnath, 1957) can be counted on for information of this nature.

Dynamic Personality Organization
in Expanded Chronologies and Vitae

Structures have so far been defined just in terms of *our* knowledge. Let us call this knowledge public knowledge (Landy, 1968).

The machine envisaged is to be one in which individuals may enter *their* programs so that these programs may also control inferences from chronoligies, vitae, and organizations just as *our* programs control those inferences. In fact, we will also speak of a machine which permits individuals to substitute personal programs for parts of ours as they grow in their understanding both of how to do so and of why doing so is personally advantageous.

In terms of the machine just described, we then trust that it is not too great a jump in imagination to consider a career machine which would contain the dictionaries and inferential programs of the individual just as they contain our dictionaries and inferential programs. Let us refer to such knowledge as private (Landy, 1968), or experiential knowledge. Such a machine could then be programmed to give to educational, job, and personal and family living events the *individual's* content as well as ours. For instance, an individual's naming of a job and the company in which it is practiced could very well be expanded by a personal description of its duties and prerogatives, the interpersonal, material, and ideational relationships it requires and permits, and the experiencing style it requires and permits in relation to the experiencing style effected in non-work environment. These descriptions could be daily ones or of longer periods of time. Normally, they would be the latter. The descriptions could also include what is hoped and planned for as well as what is taking place. Finally, the description could provide for continuous revision of past impression based on new experience and thought.

By the same token, individuals' naming of schools and subjects in their educational history could be expanded by their descriptions of the requirements and prerogatives, the interpersonal, material, and ideational relationships each has required and permitted and the experiencing style it requires and permits. Again descriptions could be recorded in minute or large periods of time. Normally they would be recorded for larger not smaller periods of time. These descriptions could also include what is hoped and planned for as well as what is taking place. Furthermore, each new recording could include revision of former recordings as new experience and impressions expand the meaning of prior events for the individual.

Finally, as has been noted when we spoke about the public organization of personality which could be conceived in one realm, then in two, and finally in any number of realms, similar conceptions of the programs for our machine would be possible in the realm of private knowledge. One realm of considerable import is that of personal and family living. Events in marriage and family formation and growth could for each such event be expanded by the individual's descriptions of its requirements and prerogatives, the interpersonal, material, and ideational relationships each has required and permitted and the experiencing style it requires and permits. Again, descriptions could be recorded in minute or large periods of time but for the moment we will imagine programs in which the period is larger, not smaller. Finally, these private descriptions could include what is hoped and planned for as well as what is taking place because our machine permits the direct entry of such personal information without needed recourse to dictionaries and inferences even though such could be personal in the case of private information. Furthermore, each new recording could include a revision of former recordings as new experience and impressions expand the meaning of prior events for the individual.

Suppose, as we did with public knowledge, we define structure in terms of the three elements: 1) requirements and prerogatives; 2) interpersonal, material, and ideational relationships required and permitted; and 3) the experiencing style required and permitted. Furthermore, suppose that in the case of private knowledge, we consider the procedures of 1) review, and 2) planning. Then the machine programs of career in the realm of private knowledge must deal with *both* structures and procedures as they produce personality organization. When we let individuals program their own descriptions of events giving rise to private structures, we allowed the association of our public linguistic framework of organization with the private procedures of review and planning. We can, of course, simulate some of this planning as Boocock (1967) has done in the case of the Life Career Game.

The machine could be programmed to use the data of the Bureau of Labor Statistics to incorporate localized and continually updated projections about opportunity in *occupations* and *education*. This program would be available in connection either with the simulation of the game or with the individuals' interactive careers describing when they are engaged in the procedure of planning. When the individuals are engaged in the interactive procedure of planning, they would also have available another machine program which allows them to find out what educational and/or occupational opportunities might be available for their *placement* in the near future.

As indicated, the machine program for dynamic personality

organization would make explicit the union of the private knowledge of review and planning procedures and knowledge of psychological processes which can themselves only be private. We shall soon say more about these important processes. We want first to enunciate a seeming difficulty we have bought in the imitation of career at the expense of introducing another's terms into our analysis.

When individuals have placed their own organization of educational, occupational, and generational events into the machine, the personal organization of each may be compared with our organization of them. This comparison is the central dynamic of personality development. We would program the machine so that the comparison is made. However, we must also program the machine with care at this point because we do not want unexamined acceptance of our terms. Instead, we want a condition in which the individual could come to realize a harmony in the personal structures of form and of experience.[3] The structures of form are both the public and private structures in personality organization. The structures of experience are both those unsimulated by the imitation career which is being constructed with the machine and those simulated by the machine including simulation of planning and practice in valuing[4] and in relating self concept and occupation.[5]

[3] This concept is due to John Wideman in Tiedeman's awareness. However, Myra Gannaway and Esther Wiedman have given the concept centrality in his concept of the imitation career.

[4] Martin Katz taught Tiedeman the importance of the conception of valuing. He is in turn developing a machine (1968) to relate the concept to educational and vocational development. Hutchinson (1967) has a procedure which makes exploration of the consequences of values possible in the predictive realm of abilities and educational or occupational rewards.

[5] Terence J. O'Mahoney is developing this procedure based on the principle of comparing and indicating preferences for vaguely defined occupational pictures judged in pairs (see O'Mahoney, 1968).

The judging of harmony in the structures of form and experience occurs in the processes of exploration and commitment[6] in career development. Hence, public developmental programs, vocational or career, must also be first programmed so as publicly to monitor these processes *in the interaction of machine and individual.* Remember that this interaction has now been programmed in our imitation career because the individual descriptions of events in chronologies, vitae, and organizations are programmed for comparison with our public descriptions of them. In the review procedure, the comparison program should foster bisociation (Koestler, 1967) between and among pairs of structures, public and private, in the several realms to be written into the machine program of the imitation career. The bisociation experience, that is the association on one plane of parts of things formerly on two planes, is a part of the exploratory process which the machine program will foster. In the planning procedure, new alternatives and their associated structures are to arise from machine programs arranged so that alternatives and structures can be under private consideration both in a condition of exploration and in a condition of tentative commitment. The difference is that in the exploration process fixation of alternative is likely to be only fleeting, while in the tentative commitment process, fixation on alternative is likely to be more enduring and also likely to lead to expansion in private structuring of one or more alternatives because of the condition of bisociation. The process

---

[6] O'Hara and Tiedeman first dealt with exploration and commitment at an implicit level in 1963. In *Career Development: Choice and Adjustment* (Tiedeman and O'Hara, 1963), they implicitly used these conceptions in an analysis of the procedures associated with decision-making in career development. Field (1964) and Kehas (1964) subsequently helped put them implicitly into the context first of purpose and then of self concept. However, it was Dudley (1966) who brought them explicitly to Tiedeman's attention in relation to the choice process. It was Segal who helped him bring them into explicit use in the definition of predicaments, problems, and psychology (1967).

of commitment is associated with the stabilization or fixation on alternatives for a sufficiently long period of time to permit implementation to occur in relation to plan for personality re-organization in career.

Obviously, the programs monitoring the processes delineated cannot now be written with any precision. Their writing remains a task of the future as relevant experience accumulates. However, this should not prevent us now conceiving their existence and in turn conceiving their revision and use on a personal basis on the part of the individuals themselves. The existence of our monitor creates the structure within which the development of agency in the personality has possibility of forming. Agency exists in the development of initiative while effecting harmony in the structures of form and experience. In the development of agency there, therefore, exists chance for the incorporation of the structure of our monitored harmonization into the personality itself. The substitution of a personal monitor for our monitor constitutes a recurrence phenomenon which is the ultimate form of the imitation career, namely the developed capacity for harmonization of the public and private forms of harmonies of form and experience. This *instrumental* sense in the imitation career brings into awareness the harmony of form and experience within the linguistics of career.

The harmonization of public and private forms and experiences represents a phenomenon suggested by Landy (1968). Landy proposes that knowledge is public and private, tacit and explicit. Tacit and explicit understanding have been further explicated by Polanyi (1956). Public and private knowledge has been defined in the imitation career. If these two dimensions are conceived as spanning a two-dimensional Cartesian space as Landy conceives them, then awareness of the phenomenon of agency constitutes the personal movement of knowledge from the private and tacit quadrant across into the public and explicit quadrant. Tarule (1968) indicates how this philosophy can be realized in the context of interest, aptitude, and achievement testing. Her stucture must therefore be a part of the machine programs creating the imitation career in the linguistic contexts of education, occupation, and generation.

Finally, machine programs in our imitation career which produce the effect of awareness in the individual cause choosing to have explicit form. In the context of choosing, educational, vocational, and generational choices themselves can have explicit existence in the mind of the individual. The patterning of the actual linguistic structure of harmony in form and experience of the individual creates personal identity. Erikson's schema (1959) of ego identity therefore becomes the final framework within which agency development must be programmed in the imitation career. This is another of the requirements for the imitation career in need of a great deal more work before the imitating of career will become much of a reality.

CAN A MACHINE DEVELOP A CAREER?

Thesis

We indicated in Chapter 5 that machines execute procedures and each machine is the embodiment of the procedure it executes. Now that we have defined an imitation career and thereby indicated the public procedures which we want a machine to embody, let us re-address the major question of this sub-section, namely, "Can a machine develop a career?" within that general meaning of machine. Let us do so in terms of three subsidiary questions, namely:

1. Can a machine develop a career *for* an individual?

2. Can a machine develop a career *with* an individual?

3. Can a machine develop a career *for itself?*

Several Meanings of "Imitation" in Literature in the Human Uses of Machines

As indicated earlier, the conception of "imitation" has several meanings in relation to our general question. One of these senses is that of simulation. In simulation, the machine is programmed to engage as much as possible in humanlike functions. Therefore, in using a machine for simulation purposes, one essentially tries to duplicate human processes. Although the question, "Can a machine develop a career *for* an individual?" may at first appear based on the argument of imitation as simulation, this need not actually be the case. Instead, our reasoning will be based on a third, and so far little used sense of "imitation," namely that of an *instrumentality* the examination of which enlightens human reasoning.

A second common sense of "imitation" in the literature on machines is that of artificial intelligence. In this sense, the machine is programmed to do things which *seem* to be intelligent. The ultimate in exhibition of intelligence is, of course, the development of programs which give the appearance of learning from past events. This is the goal which creators of artificial intelligence strive to reach. Although the question "Can a machine develop a career *with* an individual?" may at first appear based in belief in artificial intelligence, this again need not be the actual case. As indicated above, the question will be examined from a third, or instrumentality, sense of "imitation." In this third sense as it has been earlier described, the imitated is itself an instrument for an artist, or a person in general. In this usage, the instrument is actually known as an imitation and people are not therefore deluded into confusing their own processes with those of the machine. An instrument of this sort can be a powerful aid to understanding. People may reason *with* it. People can learn from reasoning with it and without danger of confusing what they can do with what the instrument can do. Richards (1955) has pointed out the value of such instruments for the study of the humanities. Career is a human product; it must be treated in human ways. Hence, as we examine the general question, "Can a machine develop a career?" we shall always be doing so while conceiving the previously specified imitation career as an instrument *with* which people may reason, not as a substitute for either their actual career or their intelligence in that actual career.

Can a Machine Develop a Career for an Individual?

The imitation career has been specified in terms of machine programs which would printout:

1) a time chronology of a work history;

2) a work vita;

3) the personality organization in the work chronology and vita;

4) the union of education and the work chronology and vita;

5) the personality organization in the education and work chronologies and vitae; and

6) the personality organization in expanded chronologies and vitae.

Specification of the imitation career in its instrumentality sense are not complete because our existing knowledge of vocational development makes it difficult to provide programs for the enlargement of a vocation into a career. However, we did note that the *Dictionary of Occupational Titles* and supporting work by the Bureaus of Employment Security and Labor Statistics makes it possible even now to infer occupation from job titles. The work of Holland and Roe also makes it possible to infer vocation and at least advancement as an aspect of career. Furthermore, their work and that of Bordin, Nachman, and Segal (1963) and Cooley additionally unite some of the childhood and educational history with the vocational history. Finally, Super's work on vocational development makes it somewhat possible to program development in personality organization.

This accumulation of what we know about programming in imitating a career in the simulation sense is not impressive. A lot of additional research is needed before we can approximate actual careers through programming an imitation career. However, there is nothing inherently impossible, from the standpoint of a machine, in developing careers *for* individuals, at least in the sense of being able to imitate a career in the instrumentality sense of "imitation." It is quite true that in our present state of knowledge, the imitation will fall far short of the actual career. However, the non-correspondence of reality and imitation is our fault, not the machine's fault.

Can a Machine Develop a Career with an Individual?

The discussion of the imitation career specified the programs which would be required to imitate the *dynamic* personality organization in expanded chronologies and vitae. That concept was developed on the assumption that a career is not just something which is written; it is something which is had. In having a career an individual comes into interaction with the part of the machine instrumentality that can write a career *for* the individual. The imitation career in its simulation sense in turn programmed this interaction so that balance in the structures of form and of experience was continually weighed by a monitoring function. However, the imitation career in its instrumentality sense let individuals substitute their monitoring function for ours as the person proved capable of writing their *own* machine which would possess the balancing effect in structures of form and experience.

As we did what we could to specify the machine programs which would simulate the things claimed for them, we took recourse in Gribbons' work on vocational readiness planning, both Crites' and Super's conceptions of vocational maturity, Katz' conception of the valuing process, and Erikson's conception of identity. That work and those conceptions offer good available approximations to the form a machine should be given to develop a career *with* an individual. However, we should again note that the present large gap in the correspondence of actual and imitated careers which persons are having is no obvious reason to dissuade us that a machine can develop a career *with* an individual. The problem is not to abandon attempts to create a simulation machine which will develop careers *with* individuals. The problem is to make our simulation machines which do so prove able to do a more effective job of it. Such improved simulation machines will still not destroy their instrumentality effect.

Can a Machine Develop a Career for Itself?

We have already argued that a machine can develop a career *by* itself. The career, of course, is not that of the machine; the career is that of the individual which the machine imitates in an instrumentality sense.

We have also already argued that a machine can develop a career *with* an individual. However, in doing so, we noted that the person had to be in actual interaction with the machine. Furthermore, we were careful to say that what was originally our monitoring by simulation of the individual's balance of structures in form and experience was gradually to be replaced by the individual's valuing of that balance. It would appear then that a machine can not actually develop a dynamic personality organization in expanded chronologies and vitae by itself. But wait, as research in the interactive functions of individuals engaged in personally determining their career progresses, we will in turn be enabled to program the machine so that it can write monitoring programs more closely approximating those written by individuals in the past. Patterning in that activity probably exists. When known, it can be turned into a machine program which will develop a career by itself, even in the second or dynamic sense of career. This will be an imitation career in the artificial intelligence sense of "imitation" as well because it will then become a self-correcting program.

Before despairing for humans, however, carefully note that this argument based in the recursion argument collapses in its limit. There will *always* be some stage of the recursion in which more experience must be accumulated in the present in order to make the machine be more effective in the future when the programming is done on the basis of prediction. Thus, although the above forms of argument get us far down the road toward believing that a machine can write a career for itself in the sense of artificial intelligence, we still have not fully addressed the question, "Can a machine develop a career for *itself?*"

In its most general form, the question, "Can a machine develop a career for *itself?*" essentialy asks, "Can programs be written for the machine which will have the effect of *giving* the machine a career?" If we can determine to what extent we can generalize the programs in which the machine develops dynamic careers *by* itself in the artificial intelligence sense of imitation, we can determine to a greater and greater extent what a machine does when it develops a career *for* itself. Doing so would considerably advance the language and ultimately the theory of career development. However, it would not of course either substitute machine careers for human careers nor deny the sense in which the imitation career is an instrument, not a master. Since we have argued by recursion, not by direct logic, we know that the esoteric career will still exist. The imitation career can only in turn make it better understood, publicly and privately.

The Value of the Question

We trust that the value of the question, "Can a machine develop a career?" now has some balance of its form with your experience. If so, you will probably attribute value to the question. If not, we have not yet proved convincing. To those not yet convinced, we can merely list here the value which the question has had for us.

In examining the question, "Can a machine develop a career?" we first had to specify the imitation career as an instrumentality in career development. In specifying the instrumentality of career development, we therefore moved the language of career development into explicit form so that it may now be investigated by anyone. We have also indicated how we fit the vocational development work of Bordin, Nachman, and Segal and of Holland, of Roe, and of Super into that instrumental framework. We additionally indicated that, with our procedure and more research, we can later provide machines which will probably do a pretty fair job of developing careers for individuals in the simulation sense of "imitation." Furthermore, we have indicated that with use of that research we can in turn start doing a reasonably good job of providing a machine which will develop careers *with* individuals in the instrumentality sense of "imitation." While doing that we also succeeded in explicitly defining processes of exploration and commitment in career development. Finally, we have indicated that several years or so of doing the latter could in turn give us a machine which would do a fairly effective job of developing careers for itself in the artificial intelligence sense of "imitation." However, in conclusion, we admit that we should turn the whole argument into a new set of questions in order to address more squarely the problem of generating a machine which will both develop careers for itself and counsel. Such an address really gains the admission which relaxes us all, even those really helped in their career development by machine. Machines don't actually develop an individual's career. Machines can only *help* individuals *understand* their career development. To this end machines are instruments, not masters, in career development.

Chapter 7

CAN A MACHINE ADMIT AN APPLICANT TO CONTINUING EDUCATION? SELF-CORRECTION AND COLLABORATIVE PROCEDURALIZATION[1]

PROCEDURALIZATION AND SOCIETY

ISVD assumed that something can be computerized without fully proceduralizing it. In Chapter 5, we indicated how the ISVD could use this notion to provide a counseling environment, namely an environment in which people have responsibility for proceduralizing that part of their decision-making development not computerized by ISVD. In Chapter 6, we indicated how the ISVD could proceduralize career as an imitation career. We concluded our consideration of that problem by noting how the machine capacity to develop careers for and with individuals and by itself can probably be improved. However, we still carefully noted that construction of machine capacity for the improvement of career development basically requires individuals who can sense the ISVD career machine as an instrument improving their *own* comprehension of their careers because of the counseling environment in which the ISVD career imitation is embedded.

The development of responsibility for one's own career can never be completed in the interaction of person and machine alone. Person to person interaction is vital as well. The person to person interaction needed is both actual and virtual.

[1]This chapter is based on Project Report No. 19, "Can a Machine Admit an Applicant to Continuing Education?" by David V. Tiedeman.

The ISVD could eventually outline the actual interaction required to make the assumption of responsibility for self in career a reality for citizens in the United States. However, this actual task also requires that the virtual interaction be built into the inquirer-machine interaction as well, thereby giving preliminary form to the later personal interactions actually required.

This chapter outlines the virtual interaction among persons which will be required to facilitate emergence of belief in one's self-correcting capabilities as one grows up. However, we again do so by examining the question, "Can a machine X?" in order to continue a form which has consistency from first principles in the counseling environment. X in this chapter is taken to be the action of admission as it is offered to another presumed to have applied for entry into continuing education. The form addressed, thereby, is that of our society, namely, group renewal by new members conceived as petitioning for membership. The basic question then becomes that of satisfying the requirements of another and of considering the authority and its basis inherent between the person petitioning and the person evaluating another. The specific question addressed is: "Can a machine admit an applicant to continuing education?"

In order to free the machine from the encumbrance of unnecessary procedures arising from fashioning its programs so that they either are or act like humans, let us do as we did in Chapter 5, namely, merely examine procedures in which *the ends of the admissions officer and the ends of the machine are identical.* It shall, therefore, *not* be necessary that the *means* of the admissions officer and of the machine be identical although there is also no reason to avoid making their means alike when doing so does not needlessly encumber the machine.

PURPOSE OF ADMISSIONS
TO THE CONTINUATION OF EDUCATION

Satisfying Education when Continued

Let us take the purpose of admission to continuation of education to be the acceptance of candidates likely to prove satisfying to the goals of the institution and the rejection of all others. In short, the applicants must *themselves* become satisfied with their education *while* they are being educated. The implications of such inclusiveness are 1) that admissions officers cannot be satisfied merely that their admitted candidates are satisfactory upon admission, and 2) that the symmetry necessarily implied in *educational* satisfaction requires both that the applicants as later students become satisfied during their admission and education and that the institution as resource for enlargement of the students' intelligence be satisfied throughout the applicants' admission and later education.

If the continuation of education is to prove satisfying to the goals of the institution admitting the applicant as specified, admitted candidates who by then are students must *themselves* set goals for the institution. Students who do so give the institution chance of viable existence. Students who live by personal goals at admissions will let the institution exist so that they can in turn assume obligation during their education to live with its goals as well. Students who live the goals of the institution will both live *by* them and live *with* them. In living *with* the goals of an institution, students will become the critics of those goals and offer the institution opportunity for its perpetual change—probably its improvement as well.

Self-Correction and the Satisfying Continuation of Education

Institutions and admitted applicants will prove most satisfying to institutional goals if both are subject to expectations for self-correction (Gannaway, 1968). The basic process of self-correction is creation. Ideational creativity, the goal of education, requires students to relate themselves to personal experience and environment so that they are both tentative about some things and from time to time committed to other things. These dual conditions permit the mind to play with ideas both as wholes and as parts. The wholeness of an idea allows one to deal in theory with its conceptually divided parts. The parts of an idea allow one to experience ideational aspects of a totality in intensity necessary for comprehension of the totality. Frequently the whole suggests parts not yet envisioned. Occasionally parts coalesce into wholes as yet unimagined. Maintenance of the belief in one's capacity for self-correction affords safeguard for the fact of self-correction. Since any belief is itself personal and inseparable, this belief like all beliefs must be *experienced* as a whole although *we* can encourage its emergence by our partial action.

The maintenance of the sense of self-correction makes demands on applicant and institution alike. For the institution, the belief means 1) that a significant portion of its officers are capable of self-correction, and 2) that the organization of the institution does not contradict the expectation for self-correcting activity on the part of such enlightened officers. For the applicants this means 1) that they must be given opportunity to share in goal determination of the institution even at the time of their admission, 2) that they must perceive this opportunity as fairly offered and fairly administered, and 3) that they must be capable of self-correction at their admission and throughout their education in the institution.

Science and Self-Correction

Self-correction is the attitude foundational to science, as well as to personal development. We, therefore, further elaborate meaning of self-correction in personal development through consideration of the more commonly understood principles of science. We refer, of course, to the *process* of science, not necessarily to the *products of scientists.* Informal and formal testing both are inherent in the process of science. We shall consider the role of both kinds of testing in the conduct of science.

We engage in informal testing intermittently in daily living whether we are scientists or not. Through such informal testing we sharpen in self-correcting ways our understanding of the relationship between ourselves and our experience and environment. Scientists additionally formalize such thought, or test in which they are willing to think one way or another depending on the outcome of an observation contingent upon a prior supposition, and call it "doing science." Scientists "do science" with concepts they have formed about their relationship between themselves, their concept, and the experience which they are attempting to understand by means of their concept. This idea about science is not novel. Polanyi relies upon it (1966). Bronowski (1965) additionally explicitly grounds the identity of man in it.

The primary paradigm of self-correction as "doing science" is that each of us seeks clarification of the relationship between an idea we have and our experience (including others' summaries of that experience). If power is expected from this primary relationship it must be additionally studied in a secondary relationship in which we comprehend our person both as the inventor and evaluator of the concept and the agent of experience of the phenomenon under study. Actually, it is impossible to separate in experience the primary and secondary relationships; the one continually interacts with the other. It is therefore necessary to conceive the two as figure and ground in phenomenological interaction. What ordinarily eventually happens when comprehension takes place is that concept and experience are given primary position as figure within the ground which is the "I-and-concept" relationship. The processes by which this effect happens occur normally. However, it is also possible for these processes to become much more available in awareness. Furthermore, it is possible for that awareness further to sharpen decision-making activity, particularly personal responsibility for decisions. The comprehension of the process itself matures very slowly in humankinds' cognitive development. As we have indicated in our prior discussion of a Career Machine, the effect can be helped to occur sporadically throughout life. However, comprehension of the general elements of the process occurs more slowly and largely in terms which so far have only been described in metaphysical terms. However, illustrations abound in which the capacity to comprehend process has reality, even if only an illustrative reality in each of many specific instances. It does, therefore, appear to be a developed capacity of which humans are actually capable even thouth the processes inherent in the secondary differentiation seem to mature more belatedly than do the processes inherent in the primary differentiation.

Formal testing differs importantly from informal testing. The important difference is that formal testing must be conceived in public terms; informal testing can occur largely in private terms.

"Doing Science" and Formal Testing

Scientists try to bring into the public realm the understanding which they achieve because of informal tests of their concepts and experience. This advance requires that understandings which are formerly tacit must be made explicit. As scientists make tacit understandings explicit, they move them from their private realm to the public realm. As scientists move their understanding from their private realm to the public realm, they find themselves explaining not alone what they know but also the bases upon which they claim to know it. These bases as they enter the public realm become the material which others can use to examine the scientists' impression of what they understand. In the pursuit of science, those bases occasionally become formalized and serve as tests which other persons in turn apply to the relationship between concept and experience which the scientists claim they understand. As this process occurs, investigations which are formerly fluid (Schwab, 1962) or "whole" later become static (Schwab, 1962) or "partial." In static or partial investigations, the bases of understanding are kept fixed while the realms of application of those bases are varied. Static investigations therefore ordinarily expand and clarify just the limits of application of an original understanding. Fluid or whole ideation on the other hand, is ordinarily relatively free of former restraints placed on static investigations. Such freeing in turn allows concepts and experiences to be "seen" and presented in new lights. When the freeing is a superordination of previously less well ordinated static restraints, science or persons are said to progress. When the freeing is the establishment of new restraints but in a different field of awareness, science or persons are said to become diversified or the like.

Means and Ends

We have so far first argued that the purpose of admission in the continuation of education should be the acceptance of candidates likely to prove satisfying to the goals of the institution and the rejection of all others. We then argued that the sense of self-correction must be preserved if students are to achieve a continuation of education satisfying to applicant and institution alike. We finally noted that awareness of "doing science" in personal living, particularly the doing of "formal testing in science," is the aspect of self-correction critical to a satisfying education.

We undertook our specification of purpose in admission to the continuation of education so that we may now note a fundamental flaw between the way tests are presently used in admission to continuing education and the end of cultivating self-correcting activity because of admission and study in continuing education. The flaw is that applicants are not *collaboratively* involved by admissions officers in the problem of goal specification and pursuit in the admissions process. Tests by themselves offer no present opportunity to correct that situation. The Admissions Machine we specify must eliminate this flaw if it is to operate in the ISVD counseling environment.

AN ADMISSIONS MACHINE

An Admissions Machine as an Integral Part of a Career Machine

If self-correction is not to be seriously contradicted during admission to the continuation of education, admission should be carried out as an integral part of the emerging self determined and corrected career. The cultivation of the awareness of "doing science," particularly the awareness of "doing formal testing," in living could be achieved during admission to the continuation of education if the needed Admissions Machine were planned as a part of the Career Machine specified in Chapter 6.

The ISVD system would use the Tiedeman and O'Hara paradigm of decision-making in vocational development as an explicit model which inquirers would be expected to master through repeated use of the ISVD. However, more importantly, through interaction with the system and with counselors who are aware of and attempting to facilitate the more general effect, inquirers are expected to master the epigenetic *process* of decision-making development or of "doing science" itself. Inquirers having such mastery are skilled in the use of purposeful action (Field, 1968), of self-correction (Gannaway, 1968), and of "doing science" or reasoning either in the sciences themselves or in the humanities as well. (Richards, 1955.)

The Admissions Machine in Broad Outline

The existence of an ISVD Career Machine could simplify the admissions process if applicants and admissions officers both believe that the other is self-correcting and mutually decide to *share* facts and data in order to collaborate in deciding, as the admissions officer must, whether this particular applicant should be admitted to this particular institution or not. The prior uses which the inquirers had made of an ISVD would give them a means of now characterizing their decision to apply to a particular institution so that the admissions officers could with the inquirers' permission, be privy to *what* and *how* they had thought, not just that they capriciously now wanted admission to institution X. The admissions officers could examine these records for detail, complexity, integrity, and self-correcting activity. The admissions officers could also plumb the records for the goals which the applicants wanted to fulfill and for the applicants' justification that such goals could be fulfilled collaboratively at institution X with its now stated goals and existing procedures for self-correction of institutional goals.

The self-correcting processes which Bronowski (1965) and Gannaway (1968) define depend upon individuals' capacity to examine honestly and continually the relationship of themselves to their experience. When individuals are doing so they are in reality acting as scientists about their self-processes. The major issues in such an examination at the time of application to continuing education are 1) the nature of the outside as that outside is known to others, and 2) the nature of purpose (Field, 1968) as its nature can be known collaboratively to applicant and admissions officer alike. The Admission Machine should therefore contain an Admissions Game which can be used by applicants in familiarizing themselves with others' experiences about admissions to continuing education. The further widening and deepening of the context for collaborative testing action between applicants and admissions officers which will be outlined later can then help both to move the decision of admissions from its present base which is almost gamelike to a more intimate base in which the aspirations and evaluations of applicant and admissions officer are more penetratingly known to both. The instrument for such exchange would be a computer-based *interactive* admissions system, or an Admissions Machine. In such systems, admissions officers could combine both the Admissions Game and their subsidiary decisions. The embedding of game and decision bases into an interactive information exchange would naturally expand the area of application of the admissions officers' thought about applicants and their intentions and accomplishments. The use of such an extensive system would give applicants a sense of participation in admissions to their continuing education.

IMPLICATIONS OF AN ADMISSIONS MACHINE FOR TEST THEORY AND PRACTICE

Testing for Admissions to Continuing Education

Although admissions officers would gain from the availability of an ISVD-like self-correcting record of applicants' careers as noted, there will undoubtedly be additional information which admissions officers would like to have. The desired additional information would likely be both of a factual and of a test kind. The needed factual information is likely to be specific to an institution and should be planned and obtained from institutions with that expectation in mind. However, the problem of testing in a potential Admissions Machine merits further examination because it is the principal effect which ISVD sought to help inquirers internalize.

The Process of Science and Admissions Testing

The process of science contributes in two ways to admissions testing. First, it forms a means of showing what admissions testing presently is. Secondly, it suggests a model of what admissions testing might become.

Admissions testing presently takes place under static conditions. For all practical purposes, psychometricians presently conceive admissions testing merely on grounds that an institution can know what it wants and how to get it by comparing predictor indexes with the series of grades achieved by the institution's classes of the years past. Psychometricians thereby cast the admissions problem into a static mold because it is conceived as merely requiring identification of characteristics visible prior to admissions which bear the transition from pre-admission circumstances to the satisfactory post-admissions continuation of education.

The present procedure of formal admissions testing thus constitutes only a feedback loop, that is the criterion is fixed and the test and associated admissions studies provide probability data in relation to the fixed criterion. A feedback system is static so far as its restraints are concerned. However, one of the ways in which a feedback system has been moved toward a dynamic or more fluid condition in which feedforward (Richards, 1955) then starts to be available has been to use the results of feedback obtained within existing constraints to make the feedback operate to correct the direction in which an object is moving. This is the sense in which feedback operates in missile guidance systems, in power steering of automobiles, and the like. This is also the sense in which psychometricians presently construe guidance as based in existing test theory.

If the planning function of an ISVD-like Career Machine were constructed and used as an Admissions Game in an Admissions Machine, we would create a first movement from a static test system to a dynamic information-creating system. Although the static system of college admissions based in present selection tests is for the most part presently deterministic, the effects of some of that determinism can be somewhat alleviated in the students subject to it by also causing them to comprehend the "theory of the Admissions Game," as well as to take tests processed in secret by admissions officers. This is equivalent to the takeover of the public monitor by the inquirer as described in the ISVD Career Machine. Students who become expert in such a game are more likely to petition for admission to continuing education on grounds which allow them to act a little more intuitively within both the restraints of the present "game" and the operation of those restraints on their desires. This is the first stage of moving admission to the continuation of education to grounds which are more fluid or self-correcting than the existing static grounds.

Widening the Data Context in Formal Testing

It is now possible to widen the context of data processed by admissions officers without sacrifice of either accuracy or accountability. The widening can be accomplished by shifting the basis of questions from multiple response to free answer. This alternative has not in the past been fully exploited both on grounds of feasibility (it takes too long to process answers in the short turn-around time between receipt of answers and need for processed results) and on grounds of reliability (you can't get readers to agree on evaluations of responses). These objections are of a different kind and should therefore be dealt with on different grounds. The availability of computers now makes it possible in short order to process responses entered into the computer by applicants. In fact, the computer can convey its response to the applicants themselves as well as to any other party permitted access to the question-response sequence. Thus, the matter of time becomes irrelevant if we program testing so that questioning, answering, and processing are done almost simultaneously.

The other objection has to do with the reliability of evaluating free response questions. Philip Stone and associates (1966) have developed a procedure for computer recognition and response to key words in context. Fred Ferris (informal report, 1968) has picked up this processing idea and exploited it in relation to the provision of College Board test items which can be answered as problems, not as selections among previously provided possibilities. With care, it then becomes possible to write questions as problems and to provide for the processing of answers according to analyses of key words in context.

If the processing of key words in context is done while the applicants are in active interaction with computer programs, further gains become possible. These further gains are 1) that the responses identified by the computer can be relayed to the applicants before they leave the system, and 2) that they can be asked to verify or revise such identifications before they leave the system. The applicants' revisions can in turn be made a matter of record and report to the admissions officers. This procedure therefore bypasses one of the major problems of re-reliability, namely, keeping the process sensitive to what the applicants intended. An additional gain is that the computer program can also report to the applicants what they have replied in relation to its processing by the test-makers' judgment of the 1) complexity, 2) completeness, and/or 3) accuracy of their answers. What we are remarking upon here is a new form of reporting, not a reporting which merely relates to the ultimate correctness or incorrectness of a response. We are suggesting a response processed according to the numerous alternatives which surround the tackling of a problem This possibility has some exciting additional consequences. It bypasses the problem of reliability still further than that already achieved by getting the applicants in on the scoring of their responses. This time the bypass is to have the test-makers provide scoring of the responses in outside terms and then to use that outside scheme both to score the responses in their terms and to share the reports of such scoring with the applicants. In sharing the scoring report with the applicants, if the applicants notice anything awry with their score, they can report such impressions. This eliminates another issue in reliability. However, the major reliability issue in test theory has to do 1) with the sampling of questions which are included in a test, and 2) with the assessment of the possibility that the level of a person's score on a sample of test items will remain relatively constant in relation to a comparison group when both sampling of content and testing of applicant is varied. Why sample content? Why compare applicants with other applicants?

We ask difficult questions. However, in its ultimate form, sampling content is indefensible. It may prove valid with a few things like sets of arithmetical operations. However, in a real sense each question is a unique question. When different questions are placed in sets, their categorization then becomes subject to question by anyone who knows the subject. These questions are ordinarily argued in test construction committees. Placements of questions in categories are ordinarily consensually achieved, not individually held. However, the placement of questions into tests is a serious problem which probably shouldn't at all be delegated by admissions officers to test committees. Are there ways in which admissions officers can deal with such decisions themselves? There prove to be ways when the selection of questions for answer are left to the applicants and when the entire set of questions from which the applicants can draw is known to the admissions officers. If applicants are allowed to respond to questions on line with computer programs and if the processing of responses is arranged as noted above, then the record of responses transmitted to the admissions officers can be not alone the applicants' processed answers to problems (complexity, completeness, accuracy) but also general statements (in the particular admissions officers' own terms should they desire such a report) of what categories of questions were attempted and what categories of questions were not attempted.

But how then do admissions officers compare one applicant with another? This is, of course, the major question when admissions officers attempt to place the requirements for limitation of applicants into the substance of a set of applicants' responses to the universe of each of several subjects. One thing we have been attempting is prevention of a quick answer to this question. We have been trying to lead you to understand that the psychometrician's prior habits of doing a lot of the deciding *for* admissions officers are no longer necessary. It is now possible to put before admissions officers themselves a lot of the data on which test committees currently themselves act. It is additionally possible to get the data to admissions officers in forms such that it has been previously dealt with by each of the applicants to their institutions before the admissions officers are required to act upon it. Hence, we would be giving admissions officers an opportunity to form their impressions about individuals in a substance which is unsummarized prior to their receipt of it but which is available for their summarization in terms including the responses of their applicants. Furthermore, for admissions officers who want such help, it would be possible to work out computer programs partially summarizing *in terms of a test's content itself* whatever the admissions officers may themselves want.

Sharing Ends Determination in Self-Correcting Institutions

It is now possible both to widen the context of data processed by admissions officers and more fully to share the problem of ends determination with applicants at the time of their application. The first point is argued above. Let's now look at the second point.

Institutions pursue their objectives on grounds that *their* use of students who are their human resources actually benefits society. These goals and judgments on which they are advanced are currently in serious question by students. We don't mean to favor one set of goals over another. However, we do argue the applicants' rights to make an institution aware of their intended use of it as well as the reverse which has been the singular asymmetry of views upon which admissions decisions have so far largely been based. *The young individuals must come to know that their society is in them as well as they in it.* This knowledge is not readily come by in our present society in which the transfer of the societal navigation from others to each person is so solidly impenetrable in our present educational institutions. At the present time we make every effort to keep youths in educational navigational systems for a long time and then to release them, naked as it were, to personal navigational systems at the end with little or no effort to cultivate what this shift *itself* entails. This assertion is subject to debate. Nevertheless, we make it on grounds both of the present lack of extensiveness of the infrastructure we know as guidance and of the inadequacies of the theory on which guidance is practiced even in that constricted condition of availability.

If we are to improve the theory on which guidance operates, it will have to become involved in the basic substance of guidance, namely the self. We do not use the concept "self" loosely. We are aware of its history in metaphysics. We too find it mercurial. However, for our discussion, we have used Bronowski's definition (1965). That is a clear definition at any rate. Like Bronowski, in talking about the "self" we therefore talk about the *grounds* which are available to personal awareness. Unlike Bronowski, we explicitly argue that comprehension *can* be facilitated *of the processes* by which that availability occurs. This is why we are offering this chapter for consideration.

The key assumption in our belief is that self-awareness deepens and widens with the comprehension of the processes of choosing. The choice of admissions to continuing education is one context for choice. In the context of admissions to continuing education, the applicants are required to place what they know in juxtaposition with what they want. They are then in a position to advance what they want in terms of what they know using the resources of an institution of continuing education as a means for their intentions and plans. If the admissions officers are to have sufficient inkling of applicants' intentions and plans, they must have a context in which what applicants know can be advanced to them in relation to what applicants want. This conjoint pair of conditions becomes possible in a computer-based interactive exchange system such as the Career Machine. Also, this conjoint pair of conditions is better grounded if its origination occurs in the substance of free responses to problems as advocated for the Admissions Machine part of the Career Machine. However, free response to problems will not be enough. What the admissions officers should additionally seek is information concerning the applicants' ability *to form* problems, not just to solve them. If applicants can only solve problems, they tend to know and interact with the world largely in another's terms, not in their own terms. If applicants are able to form problems, they are able to react to the world in their own terms as well as in another's terms. If the admissions officers watch applicants include the views and purposes of others as they advance their own purposes, they can get a substantial view of the sets for accomplishment and for use which applicants are likely to bring to the institution with them if admitted.

CAN A MACHINE ADMIT AN APPLICANT TO CONTINUING EDUCATION? OUR CHALLENGE

In conclusion, let us return to the question, "Can a machine admit an applicant to continuing education?"

We posed the question without expectation that we would answer it affirmatively. Instead, we merely proposed that we take it seriously in order to gain new perspective on the theory and practice of testing. The created perspective started from the purpose of admission to the continuation of education as the inclusion of those likely to prove satisfying to the goals of the institution and the exclusion of others. We then expanded that purpose to incorporate the goal of self-correction and the procedures of science as means compatible with achievement of that goal as a generalized attitude.

Having proposed a purpose for admissions to the continuation of education, we outlined an Admissions Machine consistent with its attainment. Finally, we used the Admissions Machine to adumbrate the assumptions of formal testing in order to pinpoint assumptions in the theory of testing which can be changed as the practice of admissions embraces the concept of an Admissions Machine.

What we propose as necessary is difficult. We have essentially suggested that the major purpose of education is to *help* persons clarify *their own* relationship to language and experience. Admissions to continuing education must be consistent with that purpose. To have such consistency, admissions to continuing education should be offered in expectation of self-correcting activity on the part of an applicant and in an atmosphere in which the applicant will agree that such has fairly been the case.

Our proposals challenge cherished assumptions in testing and admissions to continuing education, activities which have become relatively inseparable at the present time. Testing theory is largely defined in terms of admissions purposes; admission practices largely follow test theory. However, our proposals have been accompanied by relatively explicit reasoning. New means by which the pragmatic can approach the ideal have simultaneously been proposed. The concept of a machine is the principal means of both being explicit and proposing how the ideal is within realization. We make no claim that the proposed is easy of attainment. We do not even make a claim that a machine *can* admit an applicant to continuing education. However, we do claim that examination of the question *as if* a machine *could* admit an applicant to continuing education has given us a new way to question fundamental purposes and means in admissions to continuing education. In doing so, we have exposed essential flaws in our old means, test theory itself. The flaws consist of purposes realizable by machine and not by test and of the subsequent improvement of test means by machine means.

Fundamental questioning of our purposes and means is vital in our times. To fail either to question in the terms here advanced or to act on new grounds about which we are consensually convinced will be to abandon our present institutions of higher education to new forms in which the self-correcting activity now being sought by college students will find more friendly havens elsewhere.

Section IV

INTERNALIZATION OF PROCEDURALIZATION

Section III took the basic assumption of ISVD that something can be computerized without fully proceduralizing it through three phases. In the first phase, as undertaken in Chapter 5, personal responsibility for further proceduralizing the ISVD was outlined. We there outlined the counseling environment which could be computerized in order to make personal proceduralizing possible. In Chapter 6, the second phase of the problem was outlined, namely, public specification of career so that its internalization would not contradict the ISVD assumption when undertaken in the ISVD counseling environment. Finally, in Chapter 7, we extended this argument by dealing with means whereby expectations can be advanced and explicitly acted upon without compromise either to the expectations themselves or to a specific expectation for self-correcting activity on the part of inquirers.

In this Section, we undertake further generalization, namely, generalization from the specifics of career to the essence of education. We again implicitly address the question. "Can a machine X?" However, this time our question first returns in Chapter 8 to the general level at which we started, namely, "Can a machine educate?" We address this question in relation to vocational education and to secondary education. We trust our discussion in Chapter 7 suggested that secondary education is readily generalizable to continuing education when the spirit of self-correction which we are trying to engender and perfect by way of the ISVD concept heartily exists.

In Chapter 9, we conclude by squarely turning our question, "Can a machine X," into the so far unthinkable but ever present question, "Can a machine create a person?" This time, however, we do not categorically dismiss the question negatively. Instead, we examine several avenues by which our procedures do change us by becoming a part of us. The fact that procedures change us by becoming a part of us should not dismay those of us who counsel and educate because we live the ethic that what we do as procedure may in some ways be internalized by those with whom we relate. However, the fact that such an event also occurs in adequate relationship between persons and machines such as interactive computers might dismay the faint in heart of counselors and educators among us who are unwilling to look at what they do in terms of what they seek to accomplish rather than in terms of monopolizing employment appealing to them as they now secretly do. If so, so be it. Economics presently limit the presence of ISVD on the societal scene. However, the form chosen for the ISVD remains the form of our times and as computers become more parts of homes, ISVD-like systems are going to be made available to those willing to buy them. As they do, counselors and educators must re-evaluate their occupations and their identities. Chapter 9 offers a means of doing so with what we trust is some cooling out of concern for freedom in the presence of technology. We become technology only when we don't understand it, not when it exists. Understand and promulgate ISVD-like Career Machines and you will not only be unafraid of technology in guidance and counseling; you will find that you have grown in your career development as well.

Chapter 8

CAN A MACHINE EDUCATE?
INTERNALIZATION OF PROCEDURALIZATION
THROUGH VOCATIONAL EDUCATION
AND GUIDANCE[1]

VOCATIONAL EDUCATION AND CAREER

Vocational education and manpower training presently enjoy a comfortable degree of public support in today's educational enterprise. On the one hand, citizens in the United States believe that vocational education and manpower training are means of solving immediate social woes because they provide needy persons with work skills which in turn allow them to live in the dignity of return based on competence, effort, and risk of self regard. On the other hand, citizens believe that vocational education and manpower training must also help solve the longer term problem of changing the work patterns and forms of economic return of each person so that new forms of productivity can more easily and continuously take their places in our progressing civilization. We shall argue that this latter goal requires education for *career* skills but not at expense of the education for occupation and work skills which we presently attempt in our today's vocational-technical education and manpower training.

Shortsighted citizens, politicians, and educators occasionally speak and act as if these two national vocational goals

[1]This chapter is based on Project Report No. 18, "The Cultivation of Careers through Guidance and Vocational Education," by David V. Tiedeman.

cannot be achieved simultaneously. Unfortunately, the cause of vocational education suffers from such talk and action; two necessary activities are then erroneously brought into competition with each other by unscrupulous persons who may want either one of the goals at any cost to the other.

In this chapter, we particularly address the second goal or long term goal for vocational-technical education, namely, that of changing the meaning of work for citizens. In doing so, we do not mean to detract from an immediate goal of vocational-technical education, namely, that of aiding our country's attainment of full employment. Full employment must take place just as soon as the reason and passions of citizens will permit. Nevertheless, the long view must also be enunciated, clarified, and advocated along with the imperative if the necessary is to have the force of understanding, not just that of toleration. This then is our present task, namely, to enlarge understanding of the career for the individual in order to put the imperative need of work for everyone more into perspective.

SECONDARY EDUCATION TEN YEARS FROM NOW

Let us address the matter of career through vocational education by thinking of the future. We do so in order to help us see our current activity in terms of what it might become, not just in terms of what it is. Each of us needs to get above our daily activity from time to time in order to see what is possible and needs to be done. When we attempt such a perspective, we may well simultaneously despair of attaining the possible because we think that needed changes will have to go on immediately. Actually change can take place slowly if it is directed by our existing intentions. It is for this reason that we elect to think in terms of secondary education as it might be ten years from now, not as it is now. The time necessary to accomplish the considerable change now possible to us may well make the difficult more desirable in your mind. If so, we will have accomplished our objective, namely, to make you discontent with what you do now because you see goals and means of doing a needed and better job in the future.

The mere desire to think about a high school ten years ahead presents a trap we should avoid, namely, the trap of construing secondary education in terms of a high school, or for that matter, of any school at all. But if we do not think of our subject as that of a high school, or of at least a school, how can we conceive it?

In this chapter, let us consider secondary education, not a high school. However, we need some bounds. Therefore, let us first bound our concept by age. Let us take the lower age bound of our imagined secondary education at about age 12, not age 14. However, let us not bother to bound the upper age of the concept. Secondary education shall be conceived as enjoyed at any needed and/or desired time of life once an elementary grounding exists. Thus, secondary education can more readily blend into continuing education.

By choosing 12 years as the lower age in which secondary education is to occur, we can examine guidance and psychological services associated with secondary and vocational education in terms of both the adolescent and adult periods in human development. We, of course, gain capacity to discuss education in terms of human development rather than in terms of school organization at expense of difficulty in specifying the epistemological limits which will in ten years time actually restrain secondary education with its associated career and vocational education. However, several guidelines can nevertheless be imagined with profit. For instance, let us presume that secondary education has been preceded by an education which in one of its aspects has already created skill in reading, writing, and reckoning. In others of its aspects, let us also presume that the prerequisite elementary education has provided further specific cultivation 1) of interpersonal skills and 2) of inquiry in scientific, social scientific, and humanistic realms from levels in which they are naturally initiated in childhood by the family.

DESIGNING OUR CAREER MACHINES

In our future secondary education, *individually* elected paths in the realms of science, social science, and humanities can then be presumed available to students. There will be no required courses in our secondary education. Furthermore, education is to take place in experience, not *just* in books and classes. Thus, distinctions between so-called general and vocational education in today's secondary education will have no real validity in our future High School. For all these reasons, secondary and tertiary education in our future for education will be relatively indistinguishable, education beyond elementary education will be continuing education. However, one distinction which ought to prevail is that students in our future secondary education 1) be adolescent if they are educating themselves in immediate succession from elementary education, or 2) be in presumed need of a more highly *supervised* introduction to continuing education if they are then present in secondary education after having absented themselves from education for an extended period of time. In sum then, what we presume is that our future secondary education should be reserved for those in need of an interdependent, not *completely* independent, learning experience in order further to progress in the expansion of their intelligence and career according to their own purposes. The consequence of this presumption is that either adolescent or adult students who *can* profit from highly independent study and experience will actually be in tertiary, not secondary, education.

Finally, let us imagine secondary education taking place in a Learning Resources Center, not in a high school. The present theory of guidance suggests that such an organization of secondary education is not only possible but also desirable as an improved educational experience for all. The imagined existence of such an organization challenges the mind to state both how the organization can be realized and what that realization will in turn require of guidance and psychology ten years from now.

LEARNING RESOURCES CENTER
TEN YEARS FROM NOW

Integration with Services of the Community
for a Sense of Community in Services

Learning Resources Center of the future must be of its community in two senses.

One of the senses is that the Learning Resources Center must be an integral part of community centers for health, work, government, leisure and worship. Is that a physical impossibility? No, not really![2]

An Education Machine or Mechanical Book, can have the central role in our Learning Resources Center of the future. This Education Machine will function much as today's libraries function. However, it will also be available to people at home as well as at the Learning Resources Center. It will only be at the Learning Resources Center that tutorial and/or counseling help will be available with the Education Machine. However, the Education Machine will itself be available to any qualified users who keep their qualifications valid by not getting into difficulty concerning which the machine recommends referral without further machine contact until duly reauthorized at a later time. Thus, the physical location necessary will be that for a computing facility with supporting space for tutors and counselors. This should mean that integration of this space with that for health, government and worship should not be too difficult particularly because many of the informational operations associated with those functions will themselves be computerized by the time of which we write. The association of the Learning Resources Center with facilities for work and leisure may be harder to accomplish than its association with functions of health,

[2]Readers are reminded of the degree to which career education now approximates this ideal. See, for instance, Tiedeman, Schreiber, and Wessell (1977).

government, and worship. However, we do mean to stress the necessity that these functions of work and leisure *not* be permitted to be *fully* independent from those of education. It is the present separation of education from the functions of health, work, government, recreation, and worship which causes dysfunction in people's relations with their need for community largely because of the artificial difficulty of movement from one to the other.

The Learning Resources Center must, therefore, have arbitrary barriers in social structures reduced from their present levels which cause people not to experience a second or psychological sense of community. Learning Resources Center must foster a sense of individuality in every citizen but not at the expense of a sense of community as well. However, in the future let us hope that the social sense of community can be interiorized as in Chapter 7, not exteriorized as it largely is today among the alienated who speak of "our," not their, corrupt society. It will thus become a real part of identity, not a fact of alienation as is now said to be so dominantly the case. However, the psychological sense of community cannot be developed unless it evolves as a part of basic trust. In order for basic trust to have validity, access to community by way of health, work, government, leisure, and worship must all be available when people adopt at recurring moments in life the basic attitude of education, namely, to come to know and to continue to want to know (Landy, 1968). The common good will have to have more emphasis along with an emphasis on individuality than *either* now receives if the necessary sense of psychological community is to be interiorized at all extensively.

Community resources which are truly organized in keeping with the needs of individuality—and, thereby, nurture that individuality to the generative level possible in potential for all—need in turn have no concern for healthier and sturdier communities. When individuality exists in generative form, a self-sustaining dynamic also exists; individuals help the community help individuals. Adaptation will, thereby, be moved upward in the scale of civilization to self expansion *for* self *and* others.

The Tacit Dimension and Educational Resources

As indicated to the admissions officer in particular, the primary task of an educator, in general, is to facilitate the assimilation of the known. However, as previously argued, educators risk individual freedom and responsibility when they facilitate the assimilation of the known in ignorance of the processes of knowing.

Landy (1968) finds it convenient to conceive knowledge in relation both to public and private knowledge and, following Polanyi (1966), to explicit and tacit knowledge as well. Landy then proposes that these two dimensions be imagined to span a Cartesian space in which quadrants are numbered in the customary way, thus:

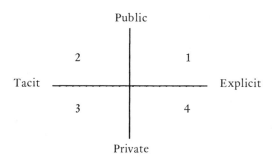

Landy first proves that knowledge exists in each of the four quadrants of the diagram. He then goes on to note that most knowledge today associated with education is in quadrant 1, the public and explicit quadrant. However, Landy argues as does Polanyi that tacit and private knowledge of quadrant 3 is interiorized knowing which is of as much importance to educational interests as is public and explicit knowledge. In fact, Richards (1955, 1968) argues that it is the potential feedforward inherent in private and tacit knowledge which actually provides the directional origin and motivational basis for knowing, the self-sustaining drive for effective curiosity.

The task of the educator is to help each student see and trust their tacit dimension. The processes and relationships inherent in education should in no way contradict the actuality and validity of tacit knowing. In fact, education should focus on *both* the explicit and the tacit dimensions of knowing; it should encourage the cultivation of tacit knowing; it should help people to achieve a discourse appropriate to their tacit processes. In this way education can encourage students to come to know and to continue to want to know, the only two valid criteria for education.

Tiedeman and Field (1965) have assessed the attention which we in the United States now give to tacit knowledge in education and personnel services. Their assessment finds such attention shamefully lacking, in fact, almost nonexistent. Their assessment is in turn associated with recommendations to the Federal government for changing Guidance-in-schools into the profession of Guidance-in-society. The recommendations associated with that assessment indicate the many great changes in conceptions, attitudes, and support which will have to occur for the revised organization to exist. We shall, therefore, not again belabor those recommendations here. We merely assume for our purposes that they *have* been followed both in the United States and Canada and that the goal of cultivating the tacit dimension in every citizen is publicly accepted ten years from now, in order that Learning Resources Center can in turn be organized so as best to realize the tacit dimension of humankind.

THE EDUCATION MACHINE
TEN YEARS FROM NOW

Individualizing Instruction by Means of
Computer-Assisted Instruction

At the present moment, we are more or less accustomed to the fact that the computer can assist in instruction. We understand this assistance largely in terms of the presentation of material and of a computer response based in whether the student's prior response has been distinguished as right or wrong We also understand that the computer can keep track of, or audit, right and wrong responses. This auditing can in turn be used to branch students to parts of the instructional programs appropriate for their present understanding of a subject.

The computer is presently used in education largely to individualize instruction. By this is meant, the placing of people in closer juxtaposition, more frequently and more consistently, with textual material considered appropriate for their present understanding. The appropriateness of this public and explicit material for present understanding is judged in terms of the rate of wrong responses they are making to queries at one level or another of the subject they are studying. In general, computer-assisted instructional programs keep people at a level until they or the program move to a more advanced level or until the subjects are inferred to be making mistakes at their present level of study at the rate of about 1 or 2 questions in every 10. When this latter inference is made, computer-assisted instructional programs then place the person with material at a presumably lower level.

Do not confuse the individualization of instruction in the above sense in which it is developed by a so-called Teaching Machine with the cultivation of individuality as it might be developed by what might be called an Education Machine or Mechanical Book. The cultivation of individuality is a higher goal in education than is drill and practice leading to knowledge assimilated in only public and explicit terms.

Although the construction of an Education Machine or Mechanical Book which will cultivate individuality is a difficult task, it is not an impossible task. In the late 1960's the United States Office of Education supported a project in which a prototype Information System for Vocational Decisions (ISVD) was under construction. As indicated in this book, ISVD is basically a Career Machine; a Mechanical Book for the realization of purpose in career development. However, it is now almost possible to turn the ISVD Career Machine readily into an Education Machine. This is an assertion of considerable importance for the creditability of our future Learning Resources Center.

A CAREER MACHINE: THE INFORMATION SYSTEM FOR VOCATIONAL DECISIONS

Detailed descriptions of the ISVD will be found in earlier chapters. Here we will focus on how conversion to an Education Machine might occur.

The ISVD would be programmed to monitor or assess the quality of the decisions that are based on the material in the data files. As specified in Chapter 2, this same monitoring process could provide the users of the System with information regarding how abstracts and the thesaurus of index terms are generated. With this knowledge, they can use the information collected during their review of the data files to construct their own thesaurus of terminology and to go on and process the information. A small, personal, esoteric information system is, thereby, created because it has also become an explicit part of the individual. The individual has succeeded in moving private and tacit knowledge into the explicit realm which could also be public if the individual elected to make it so. If the process is truly to be completed, the monitoring system within each person makes them aware that language and experience never perfectly correspond—that paradoxically, their understanding of their actions and experience cannot be perfectly construed. Perforce then, individuals learn that they must generalize when expressing and interpreting to others. Generalization also must occur when individuals convert the learning that takes place in a simulated situation to real life experiences. Counselors, using their own interaction with clients and drawing upon their skill in assessing creative processes, become the first agents of generalization. Using this same assessing skill but focusing on the substance of the individual's situational role obligation, military, school, or work supervisors become the second agent of generalization. The ultimate agents of generalization are the individuals themselves. From weakness and incongruencies that become apparent in the simulated situation, they gain realization of the knowledge and lack of knowledge in their personal guidance system and the consequences on their lives.

The ISVD could, therefore, provide the series of "dress rehearsals" which a person needs in career in order to achieve realization of self processes in the choice processes of career. Each "dress rehearsal" represents an imposed opportunity to make errors in the abstract before they become fatal. However, the proposed relationships between the inquirer and both the counselor and the supervisor represent an additionally imposed opportunity to insure that "the play goes on." The abstract must be brought into action. The ISVD Career Machine, therefore, constitutes the "instrument" (Richards, 1955) required to bring the tacit over into the explicit quadrants of knowledge. However, the human relationships also implicit in the ISVD career theory further insure that the explicit is brought from the realm of thought into the realm of action as well.

An Education Machine

The Education Machine or Mechanical Book would be constructed along the lines of the Career Machine. The attitude expected of the Education Machine's users will be that of inquiry. The basic files of the Education Machine will be those of subjects, not just that of career. The monitoring of the Education Machine will be programmed to deal with the elements of individuality which inquirers can be expected to exhibit while addressing the assimilation of a subject's structure as programmed in 1) its basic files, 2) the game-like context in which it can be reasoned with, 3) the specific contexts in which the inquirers elect to use the subject in creating their esoteric form of it, and 4) misconceptions expected during assimilation.

The basic learning in the Education Machine will be the same as in the Career Machine, namely, that language and experience never perfectly correspond. This realization will come in the Education Machine in the inquirers' experience with the subject they are attempting to assimilate; in the Career Machine, with their career they are attempting to understand and gain personal control of.

As with the Career Machine, generalization must occur when individuals convert the learning that takes place in a simulated situation into real life experience. However, in the case of the Education Machine, tutors, not counselors must use their interaction with the students and their skill in assessing creative processes in their subject to facilitate this generalization. Using this same assessing skill but focusing on the substance of the individual's situational role obligations, work supervisors, ministers, and/or family members become the second agents of generalization in conjunction with the Education Machine and the tutor.

The ultimate agents of generalization are the individuals themselves in the Education Machine as in the Career Machine. From weakness and incongruencies that become apparent in the simulated situation they gain expanding realization of the knowledge and lack of knowledge in their education and the consequences of both on their lives.

As was the case with the Career Machine, the Education Machine will, therefore, also provide the series of "dress rehearsals" which a person needs in order to achieve realization of self processes in the choice processes of any subject. Each "dress rehearsal" represents an imposed opportunity to make errors in the abstract before they become fatal. However, the proposed relationship between the inquirer and both the counselor and tutor represent an additionally imposed opportunity to insure that "the play goes on."

CAREER RESOURCES
AND THE LEARNING RESOURCES CENTER

The section on the Career Machine specifies the reasoning processes involved in career development which should be a part of everyone's education. However, there are vocational and social skills involved in career which also require attention and cultivation.

Today's vocational literature abounds with advice that people will in the future have not one but many jobs in their lives. In the future, people must, therefore, have not just an *occupation*; they must have a *vocation*. As Morley and Tiedeman (1966) have writeen, *vocation is an individually derived theory of employment which lends continuity to a person's several occupations and many jobs as the person thinks about both together*. There are many implications of such personal knowledge for the secondary educator, particularly the vocational educator. Some of these implications were pointed out by Gross (1966) who advocates that the study of social and personal skills be incorporated into the curriculum in a modernized vocational education. These implications are also appearing in some of the better projects organized under terms of the Manpower Development and Training Act and its successor, the Comprehensive Employment Training Act. In these better MDTA and CETA projects, education in social and personal skills accompanies education in work skills. By the above definition, education in social and personal skills is a part of vocation. Hence, it should also be construed as a part of an improved vocational education. This is the first assumption underlying this effort to bring a new potential in career education into secondary education.

People who both know how to work and how to operate in the social and personal environment of work have acquired the theory of a vocation as Morley and Tiedeman define that theory. They are also well on their way to understanding both the personal and *common good* which is a part of the individuality sought in our future secondary education. However, there is still a more highly developed form of vocational capacity, namely, career competence. Career competence represents for work the actual individuality which ISVD seeks. *A career is both a sequence of jobs linked in the continuity of personality by the person, a vocation in short, and a sense of one's responsibility and initiative in that vocation.*

The sense of personal responsibility and initiative in one's vocation as defined is not readily attained. In fact, it is a lifetime attainment which is always in flux, never complete. Nevertheless, the *feeling* that one is in control is a natural feeling capable of awareness. It is humankind's singular characteristic of their humanness.

There are two elements of this *feeling* of being in control which are extremely relevant to career capacity or career development. One of the elements is the objects, ideas, or goals themselves which one controls. This element arises internally as feedforward (Richards, 1968). *Feedforward is that existing but unarticulated sense of something you are trying to bring into being*, a poem in the making, a new development, a vocation, or simply your present understanding of what we hope is now at least a vague idea of yours, not just ours alone. The second element of the feeling of control which is relevant in career development is the sense of responsibility and initiative one feels *toward oneself and others* as one works to articulate one's feedforward. It is this sense of responsibility and initiative *for* one's vocation, or *a sense of agency* which is the prime subject of guidance and psychological services in our future Learning Resources Center. An effectively functioning sense of agency in each citizen will bring us to a new level of existence, a level in which individuality functions for personal *and* common good.

IDENTITY AND THE LEARNING RESOURCES CENTER

Adolescence and Identity

Erikson (1959) fixes the crisis of identity in the adolescent period. This is why we chose the period of adolescence as the lower bound for secondary education in our future Learning Resources Center. Adolescence brings with it many bodily changes which find expression in the socio-psychology of people as they educate themselves. It is a period when adolescents strive to find and to assume a position in life which they want. The outlined Education Machine contributes to the ideological growth which grounds and determines identity during the period. The outlined Career Machine also grounds this burgeoning ideological identity in the dimensions of job, occupation, vocation, and career. The career skills which have also been described add the social context in which identity forms. However, the Learning Resources Center must rely upon interactions with people to round out the emerging identity in adolescence.

A Sense of Agency in Career and a Sense of Identification

Every citizen must actually achieve this higher level of individuality in our progressing civilization. The ISVD Career Machine set in the context for career skills in Learning Resources Center holds promise of permitting achievement of this aim in the future. However, integration of community resources for the common good, individualization of instruction, and education for individuality must all be tempered in the fostering of identification, the fundament of identity.

The society of our future Learning Resources Center will be without many of the overt structures in which we were raised and have so far raised our children. These overt structures have furnished guides for social expectations, models to be envied, and pathways for entry and progress. The Learning Resources Center of the future will attempt to move these structures from external to internal bases. The ISVD Career Machine could attempt to do this by providing an overt linguistic framework within which people can know the balance of authority of form and of experience which they create for themselves and use as their cue for satisfaction in acting responsibly while striving. The Education Machine could generalize this effect in other subjects. However, the primary difficulty will then move from one of present feeling of cramped opportunity to one of future feeling of missing limits. There will be too little societally built-in feedback provided by fulfilling the expectations of others.

The Teaching Machine in the image of present kinds of computer-aided instruction could furnish one set of limits for expected form in experience. The Career Machine and its companion Education Machine could set other kinds of limits, particularly those having to do with the origination of intention and the evaluation of progress in intention. Finally, counselor and tutor would be models and cultivate generalization of purposeful action in all realms of living. However, the Learning Resources Center of the future will additionally have to foster all kinds of contact of students with persons whom they may be attempting to emulate, initially probably unconsciously. This contact could first be in the form of vivid sound movies and the like. The contact can then be further augmented by the provision of game-like conditions in which acts can be undertaken and in which consequences can be experienced seriously but without real harm. But simulated experience will have to give way to real experience as quickly as possible in order for the authority of experience to have adequate play in balancing people's authority of form as they strive. This requirement then merely underscores the already stated need for setting the Learning Resources Center into the entire set of services in its community. This is the way that models of envy, simulation, and excellence can be shared both with adolescents who are aspiring to do and with adults who are seeking new careers.

Learning in Experiencing

Identity is ultimately forged in the crucible of action. It is in action that individuals are both ultimately themselves and subject to the evaluations of that self by others, others to be sure who have come to mean much to them, to paraphrase Erikson (1959).

These facts provide additional reasons why secondary education should take place in a Learning Resources Center, not in a school. A Learning Resources Center offers the flexibility required for an andragogy based in a learning of experiencing, not in a learning of telling. As long as there are figures for identification, facts which can be turned into information in the crucible of action, and expectations for excellence, we need have no fear that our future Learning Resources Center will continue the knowledge of our civilization. Instead we can derive hope that learning will also more regularly become a living part of a person's personality, that career can become personally determined, not externally imposed, and that life can be based as much in satisfaction as in success, a balance right now hardly ever even considered. Individuality will become more of a universal reality. However, it will be an individuality based in mutuality, not in selfish independence.

Other Careers

We have specified that future secondary education was for adolescents if they progressed into it without a needed period of moratorium and for adults who needed an education based in other or additional social as well as ideological development. We trust that the discussion of identity above makes it clear why secondary education for identity is as appropriate for adults starting other careers as for adolescents starting their first careers. The context of individualized instruction by way of the Teaching Machine, of the Career and Education Machines, of career skills, and of a community of service for a sense of community in service is the context creating additional as well as initial careers. These are the conditions in which identities are born and nursed until healthy enough to exist independently.

MENTAL HEALTH, EDUCATION AND THE TREATMENT OF MENTAL ILLNESS TEN YEARS FROM NOW

Psychology and Mental Illness Ten Years from Now

Mental illness cannot be exactly estimated, because definitions and understanding are both highly amorphous. Nevertheless, at the present time, a rate of about one mentally-ill person in every ten persons is ordinarily accepted as a reasonable rule of thumb. We have no reason to assume that this rate will dwindle, even with our future Learning Resources Center. Hence, let us plan pessimistically expecting mental illness at this high rate, thereby, not blinding ourselves to its probable continuing existence.

It is a moot point as to where the locus of mental illness rests. There is clear evidence that the psychogenic hypothesis concerning the confused mental state holds in a substantial fraction of cases of mental illness. However, there is also growing evidence that blood changes are at least associated with, and may even be causing or be caused by, severe psychotic states. For this latter reason, chemotherapy for mental illness should be expected to be in a highly advanced state within ten years. This will mean that the psychologists in our Learning Resources Center will either have to be trained better in medicine themselves or to rely more heavily on the community resources in medicine. They can do the latter if health and education are joint functions in a community center in which our Learning Resources Center exists.

Among those cases of mental illness in which the psychogenic hypothesis seemingly still holds good, there is also growing evidence that the confused mental state is grounded in people's family, society, and culture as much as in themselves. These realizations are giving rise to new forms of social treatment which focus upon the community and the healthfulness of its climate as resources in curing mental illness.

The new social treatment of mental illness is taking two major lines in its present development. On the one hand, electronic monitoring devices are being placed in the body or on the person of a mentally ill patient. Such patients are then permitted to roam their community while their psychological state is being continuously monitored at a central receiving center. This treatment permits patients to live a somewhat more normal life until an acute psychological episode becomes somewhat imminent, in which event they are warned to hospitalize themselves or are brought into hospitalization if for any reason they cannot do so or refuse to heed the warning.

The second direction which the new social treatment is taking leads to the encouragement of sociability, further education, and employment. This form of treatment recognizes that health is predicated on coping ability in human relationships and on economic independence.

Both of these lines of social treatment are likely to expand and to improve in the next ten years. Therefore, psychologists in the Learning Resources Center of secondary education in the future might well be intimately involved with elctronic monitoring of students' psychological states in its medical wing and with secondary prevention of mental illness through both education and employment counseling along with its Career Machine. The psychologists engaged in educational rehabilitation of the mentally ill students will also probably find themselves needing to use behavioral therapy as a technique. This behavioral therapy cannot of course engender the desired individuality; it can only create conditions in which individual choosing once again becomes somewhat more possible. Therefore, since the use of behavioral therapy is essentially antithetical to the sense of individuality our Learning Resources Center of the future is attempting to create, we must limit its use to extreme cases and continuously attempt to minimize the risk that reattainment of the necessary curiosity which underlies choosing is then erroneously accepted by the person helped as the actuality of choosing.

Psychology, Guidance, Education, and Mental Health in the Learning Resources Center

The mentally ill will be educated in the Learning Resources Center to the extent that their confused mental conditions permit education at any given moment. However, as Tiedeman has argued (1961), the primary prevention of mental illness requires an educational, not a medical stance.

The guidance activities outlined in conjunction with the cultivation of career and of a sense of agency in learning foster mental health in our future Learning Resources Center. The services provided by counselors in such primary prevention of mental illness and those therapeutic activities of the psychogists undertaken in interest of secondary prevention of mental illness are both based in the functioning of the ego. However, the psychologists are primarily involved in the reconstruction of belief in one's own curiosity which is required if choice is to take place at all. The counselors for their part are involved with that same curiosity at the time when the structures of choice are actually being formed, within it. Furthermore, counselors are involved in bringing into awareness the fact that choice is and should be taking place.

These conditions underscore the necessary joint reliance of psychology and guidance on ego processes. It also suggests that the two are intimately associated by their common interest in curiosity and choice processes. However, therapy in mental illness makes education possible. The cultivation of purposeful action in counseling makes education effective. Therefore both psychological and guidance services will be present in the Learning Resources Center. Both counselor and psychologist can do the same things in that Center so long as each also does the distinctive things dictated by differentiated conditions. However, the presence of the Education Machine or Mechanical Book and its supporting tutor will round out the triumvirate of functions necessary not only to educate and to make education effective, but also to make education contribute in the expansion of our civilization.

Chapter 9

CAN A MACHINE CREATE A PERSON?[1]

EDUCATION IN A MACHINE CONTEXT

The development of computer systems for use in vocational guidance, as in other areas of education, is under way. Their continued and expanded use is as inevitable as it is both necessary and desirable. Answering the questions of what is and can be the role of such machines in the educational future can be facilitated by asking *in a machine context* the essential questions of how people learn, how they interact with any part of the environment—machine or otherwise—and what are the far-reaching goals individuals entertain in devising systems of education. This chapter calls for a fresh defining of terms by those who would develop Career Machines and by those who will sit down at them; for counselors must be prepared to deal with both new kinds of machines and new kinds of people, as education moves further into a machine context.

There was a time when any machines associated with school were to be found only in the industrial arts department or the business department, if there. Now schools are being affected by the computer revolution: machines schedule courses for an entire student body and provide data about occupational and academic opportunities. But computers are, of course, machines capable of uses beyond the sorting and

[1] This chapter was written by Douglas A. Dunlap, a counselor at Rough Rock Demonstration School, Chinle, Arizona and Guidance Intern of the Harvard Graduate School of Education at the time of writing.

vending of data. What is their relationship—and their potential relationship to the inquirers' learning processes and their active and interactive relationship with their environment—machine or otherwise? What are machines capable of doing? What are people capable of doing?

On the eve of widespread application of machines to institutions' instructional, guidance, and education work, we raise such questions. In doing so, we seek an understanding of what future people will be like, as well as their machines, and the implications for future education.

Our point of reference is the Information System for Vocational Decisions. As indicated, the ISVD was a proposed computer-based guidance system that endeavored not only to provide essential data for vocational and other decisions but also to foster a personalization of knowledge for decision-making. This system was one of a number of vocational guidance endeavors employing machines that demand interactive involvement from those who use it. The development of such systems requires examination of the person-machine relationship. The challenge is not only how to build machines; it is also how to *view* them.

Albert Camus, writing his preface to **L'Envers et L'Enfant** in 1958, provides a starting point for the problem of conceptualizing machines:

> Naturally, a writer has some joys he lives for and that do satisfy him fully. But for me, these come at the moment of conception, at the instant when the subject reveals itself, when the articulation of the work sketches itself out before the suddenly heightened awareness, at those delicious moments when imagination and intelligence are fused. These moments disappear as they are born. What is left is the execution, that is to say, a long period of hard work.

This is a chapter about such delicious moments: about how persons and machines learn and define themselves from one

CAREER DEVELOPMENT

another, about how a changing machine can work with a changing person in those moments when public and private, imagination and intelligence join, about creation and how education can be synonomous with creation. It also represents one of those delicious moments.

Robert Coles (1967) has suggested that people have abstracted two lives from the universe: the life of the mind and the life of the world. But although people have abstracted these in an effort to conceptualize the universe in manageable pieces, Coles maintains that there is an intense continuity that is shared by the two lives. In fact, they do come together at times, such as during the moments of crisis he studied during the school de-segregation endeavors in the South in the early nineteen-sixties. People struggle to make the complicated and difficult connection between the two lives; and at certain delicious times they fuse. When they are at one, there exists the act of creation.

The theme of this chapter is creation. The title question "Can a Machine Create a Person?" places person and machine on either side of "creation." The question essentially is how to move from one to the other in the experiencing of the act of creation. But what is creation? We offer no singular definition; only various indications and impressions that there is something that can be called creation. The sense that creation is coming and that it has taken place—the feedforward and the feedback—the sense that creation is present, as in Camus' moment of conception and heightened awareness; these we must offer in lieu of a definition of creation itself.

In Chapter 5, Ellis and Tiedeman write that "Art imitates nature in the processes of production as well as in the objects produced." They make this statement in the context of a discussion of the meaning of imitation. We wish to extrapolate from these remarks the suggestion that the creation moment for persons occurs when human activity (art) becomes at one with the life of the world (nature). The two join in a flash, they are the same and of the same. Then they part, "disappear as they are born" in Camus' words; and people struggle to recapture them, not understanding the creation, only chasing the shadow of that delicious moment.

Camus also wrote in the Preface to **L'Envers et L'Endroit** that "I know with certainty that a man's work is nothing but the long journey to recover, through the detour of art, the two or three simple and great images which first gained access to his heart." What are those images? Are they the images of creation? If so, we are bound for a journey of hard work, the execution: the quest for the re-uniting of the life of the world and the life of the mind. Can machines help? With people, perhaps they can.

PEOPLE AND MACHINES: OVERVIEW

Are the machines that people have devised going to take them over? Do machines control people? These questions, popular with science fiction writers, have a poignant relevance today, with the growing use of computers, that they have not had before. Such questions point to two main issues that we consider in this chapter. The first issue is the question of what has been created in a given machine besides that for which it was intended. Have people placed in computers possibilities that they do not realize are there? The second issue is the question of the relationship between people and machines, as the latter become more complex and sophisticated.

Our thesis is that people, like machines, are changing and becoming more complex and sophisticated. Or, more concisely, the definitions that are held of the two are changing. The distinction that we make between persons and the definition of persons is between what is unknown and what is known, what persons can be and what they are. How do humans move from what they are to what they can be? What is the process by which the definition of humanness becomes expanded? It is the process by which people learn. Then we must ask "How do people learn?"

Abraham Maslow (1965) has distinguished two kinds of

learning: intrinsic and extrinsic. Erich Fromm (1947) made a similar distinction between generative and reproductive experiencing of the world. A look at their distinctions and definitions provides a feeling for the kind of learning essential to how people move from what they are to what they can be.

Extrinsic learning Maslow explains as the behavior or acquisition, of collecting things, perhaps the memorization of a date or a formula. Fromm's conceptualizing of reproductive experiencing of the world takes that behavior to be photographic: a literal record of things experienced. Things are seen as they are or as they are perceived to be by a person's culture. Reality is a sum of what has materialized, been photographed, and stored. The learning represented by these difinitions is one of acceptance by a self that is minimally involved, if at all, in any active way with what is being learned or learned about.

Intrinsic learning involves another dimension. Maslow sees it as involving the processes of "learning to be the best human being you can be" and describes the far goals of education as "the ways in which we can help people to become all they are capable of becoming." Fromm speaks more specifically of his generative experiencing: it involves conceiving of the world and enlivening and re-creating it through the spontaneous activity of a person's own mental and emotional powers. Such perspectives as these embody the kind of learning with which we are concerned; they reflect the dimension of humanness that we are considering in this chapter.

How can learning be related to a machine? In creating a machine people are also adding to their environment. People add an element from which they *will* learn, and from which they *can* learn more than what they originally placed in the machine. A way of looking at this person-machine relationship is to take the example of a person-confronting machine that has been designed for purpose X. Assume that people have no prior knowledge of this machine. People can learn X, all that the machine was designed and built to do. They can learn X-minus, part of the machine's designated function.

They can learn X-plus, what the machine was designed and built to do plus something that people perceive in the machine that its creators did not see. There are other possible combinations: people can go directly to a plus perception of the machine without knowing X; or they may have an X-minus and a plus combination. Learning—intrinsic, generative—occurs when there is interaction with the environment such that there is expansion upon, deliverance of, or giving of definition to, the "stuff" that is within people. This stuff is the potential, the unknown, the mass of rock out of which emerges the sculptured person. Education moves from the inside out, not from the outside in. The role of the outside—and that outside can include machines—is in calling upon what has hitherto remained inside and undefined.

That there is more in the machine that can be learned than was purposely placed there broadens the scope of the learning that can be taking place in a machine context. For people do not learn only from what is known to be in the machine; they also learn from what *can* be there. But what is the something that is unknown but yet exists in the machine? Robert O'Hara of ISVD once remarked in a class that there is more flexibility in the system than was thought originally. What does this mean? Consider, for example, that a machine built to add and subract is also capable of multiplying and dividing for the latter two functions are forms of the first two respectively. This is a particularly poignant example for two reasons. First, it provides a metaphor for programs involving something other than simple arithmetic, like a Career Machine. Second, addition and subtraction are the processes by which many computers physically operate, regardless of program. Thus multiplying and dividing are both theory and realizable practice.

The person-machine relationship is not a one-way learning relationship. Let us turn the proposition around and suggest that the machine, too, interacts with the environment and learns not only what is there, but what is potentially there. Just as the machine enlarges in definition through people's interactions with it and draws upon its potential, so, too, can the machine interact with the people to draw them out, to re-define, to create humans. Here enters the initial question "Can a Machine Create a Person?" For as people develop machines they will not remain static. While humans' creations grow they will interact with the machine to grow and re-define themselves, and in this sense be created by machines. An alternative way of viewing this proposition is to say that people are human because of the way they interact with their environment. This interaction distinguishes them from other creatures. This is a functional definition of humanness. Now that human's environment comes to consist more and more of machines it will be machines more than other aspects of the environment that will come to define or create persons.

THE MYTH OF THE MACHINE

> As I was going up the stair
> I met a man who wasn't there.
> He wasn't there again today.
> I wish, I wish he'd go away.

Hughes Mearns, The Psychoed

Computers call up a fear of the unknown. A popular myth is that computers can be made to be human-like. We know already what excesses humans are capable of; it is little wonder that a human-like computer represents a fearsome unknown. Although the term "electronic brain" seems to have been discreetly dropped from usage and replaced by "computer," still the idea that a machine can have human powers—or greater—lingers.

Arthur C. Clarke, in his science fiction story 2001: A Space Odyssey, has raised dramatically the question of the relationship of people to highly sophisticated machines. In Stanley Kubrick's motion picture version of 2001 there is a computer on board a space craft that (who) directs the craft's mission. This machine carries a name, Hal (i.e. IBM minus 1), speaks English, has feelings that it (he) discusses with human crew members, and is able to plan and execute murder when it (he) feels threatened. The viewer of this motion picture is impressed as much by Hal's ability to converse and participate in games with the crew as it is with its (his) ability to monitor the physical operation of the space craft, navigate, and so on.

Clarke has told a good story. What has he said about people and machines? He has surely stretched the imagination in his presentation of Hal, and raised in a very powerful way the question of the relationship of people to the highly sophisticated machines that they are proceeding to build. Although in 2001 people win the final round with the computer, Hal is considered to be superior to men, whether in calculating fuel supply or in playing checkers. The crew member who dismembers Hal in the end does not seem to be so superior or sophisticated in his human-ness as does Hal in his machine-ness. The man wins by being tricky, and that cleverness does not seem the equivalent of superiority. Who wants to live constantly being called upon to outwit machines in order to survive? And in 2001 even the victory is small indeed, for the mission was dependent upon the computer!

This conversation about 2001 is of heuristic value. Our complaint about that story is that its people appear too small beside the machines, that fantastic people do not appear alongside the fantastic machine, that one has been presumed not to grow while the other has "grown." We raise the question of whether remarkable Hal could have been created by people who were not themselves remarkable.

Are we suggesting that there is no danger of machines taking control? (That question is too loaded for a response.) There is some kind of control, perhaps more accurately defined as dependency upon the machine to perform a particular function. We become used to employing a machine for certain purposes, and if the machine were not available such purposes could be more difficult or even impossible to

CAREER DEVELOPMENT

achieve. This means that the machine does somehow "control" human behavior. But are the controls placed upon people by sophisticated machines different relatively from the controls that exist at the present time—or have existed at any given time in history? Are we concentrating too much upon the machines that will exist in future years and not giving enough credit to the people who will live in those years?

We presuppose a state of stasis between people and the environment. As the environment comes to involve more machines, people will relate more to a machine environment. People are defined as such because of their relationship to their environment. The environment is not static; hence, neither are people. A machine is as valid a part of the environment in its interacting-creating-defining influence on people as is any other aspect of the environment. We examine this interaction in the next section.

A final word on machine "control." We do not contend that machines do not exert any serious challenges to humankind's position. In fact, without challenges from machines we do not see how people could grow in relation to machines. Certain machines seem to dictate the pattern of daily life. But, again we must be clear about what control means.

The machine is only a machine. (This is supposed to be the equivalent of saying that a person is only human.) The myth of the machine, the control issue, taking over—these are spurious issues. People have a relationship to machines that is not beyond humankind's means either to understand or to affect. Let us look closer at that relationship.

THE MACHINE AND THE ACT OF CREATION

What are the elements of a creative act that occurs in a machine context? Can a machine create a person?

We approach these question by asserting that an essential quality of creation or of a creative act is the giving of definition to some unknown "stuff" such that this stuff becomes known. This is explicit knowing, as Michael Polanyi (1959,

1966) has divided knowing into *implicit* and *explicit*. This knowing can involve seeing, hearing, physical feeling, smelling, tasting, measuring, verbalizing, thinking. We assume that there is no sound until there is an ear, no weight without measurement.

Creation involves the bringing into existence of the measuring device that makes it possible to recognize or define something that previously did not exist because there was no way to sense it, receive it (in the radio sense), deal with it. In order for X to exist there must be a way to sense X-ness. An alternate way of expressing this idea is that there must be a purpose attached to X in order for X to exist. Polyani (1959) offers the following connection between meaning, which is another form of existence, and purpose:

> Symbols can serve as instruments of meaning
> only by being known subsidiarily while fixing
> our focal attention on their meaning. And this
> is true similarly of tools, machines, probes,
> optical equipment. Their meaning lies in their
> purpose; they are not tools, machines, etc.,
> when observed as objects in themselves, but
> only when viewed subsidiarily by focusing
> attention on their purpose.

A person who pounds a nail using a wrench creates through purpose. The person who uses computer A for purpose B is doing the same thing.

But what is the stuff, the X, that is waiting to be discovered, like so many stars sprinkled beyond the range of our most powerful telescopes? Is there any evidence of potential existence, of non- (not yet) existence?

In **The Act of Creation**, in a chapter entitled "Learning to Think," Arthur Koestler suggests that human beings program the environment so that we have certain things we look for, and these things in turn are what we perceive. He writes: "Thus all along the line we abstract and discriminate only qualities which are relevant to us; and new discriminations arise as a result of changes in our criteria of relevance . . . " In this context, *it is what is known that is relevant.* That is what we look for and ask about; therefore, it is what we find. We abstract and define only those qualities that are known. What is known at any given point in time is only part of all that is potentially knowable.

Koestler provides a handle for the problem of dealing with knowns, unknowns, and knowables, in his discussion of language. Language lags behind experience. "Words cannot describe," people are prone to say, and they *can't*. Take the example of learning a second language and discovering that there are ideas or feelings that can be expressed in one language that cannot be expressed in another. The second language in such a case is a device that defines feelings that were less than known before this language, an ear, a vehicle for discovery, brought them into being or created them. Our society places a high value on the ability to articulate feelings—on great poets, authors, and speechmakers. Such persons may possess the ability to bring into being feelings that less than completely existed for people until these feelings were placed in a form that rendered them recognizable—in this case until they were verbalized.

"What needs stressing," writes Koestler, "is that words are symbols for perceptual and cognitive events, but they are not the events themselves. They are the vehicles of thought, but the vehicle should not be confused with the passengers." He speaks of a "dawn of symbol consciousness," and we suggest that humankind never really gets very far beyond this point, this dawn state. People are continually and endlessly devising and learning symbols in order to deal with events, but because these symbols can never be equated with the events, the process never ceases. It is never completed and it never stops uncompleted.

There is a Sisyphus quality to the process, for as each new symbol is devised its inadequacy is also recognized. There is an increased awareness of more remaining that is unknown.

The symbol searching process goes on. This is not a hopeless process. It is the dynamic process of life and of growth. The goal of education is process, and the understanding that life *is* process.

If we can acknowledge that learning to speak is a process of taking that which does not exist in a way that can be dealt with and defining it in such a way that it *can* be dealt with, we have a handle for understanding the interaction-creation potential of a machine. Learning to speak assumes that there are things unverbalized that can be verbalized. By claiming that there is potential in a machine for people to discover new ears or eyes or language, we assume that there *are* things unreceived or unsensed that can be sensed. We don't know what they are because we don't have any way to receive their signals. If we did they would not be things unsensed, they would be things!

What role can the machine play in creations? It is difficult to answer that question without further examining the nature of the stuff, the unknowns, the potentially knowable. Is there any way to accept these potentials other than on blind faith? A discussion of feedforward as it relates to machines is in order.

FEEDFORWARD AND TACIT UNDERSTANDING IN A MACHINE

In "Learning to Speak" Koestler writes that "Before the verbal hierarchy is set into motion, there is an ideational process of a highly conscious character, an intention or active expectation, which itself is not yet verbalized." "The knowledge of an approaching discovery" is how Polanyi describes this process. It is the feeling, the anticipation, undefined and unverbalized, that something is going to *be*. Consider that there is a certain energy in the anticipation, in the tacit understanding that creating and defining is imminent. The energy represents, in the words of Ivor Richards (1968), "some sort of preparation for, some sort of design arrangement for one sort of outcome rather than another . . . " Feedforward, the energy of feedforward, represents a middle stage in creation.

There is a middle stage that brings an unknown to a point where a receiver is now being built for it; because it is known that there is something "out there." (The limits of language in this discussion are truly exasperating—an excellent example that there are unknowns that have entered our tacit-knowing stage but still remain to be yet defined-created!) It is this stage where people become alert to the fact that there *is* something potentially to be created. Its existence is crucial, for feedforward in its own way creates in its stage the potential that is about to be defined-created on the cognitive level. Just as the existence of a set of scales insures that we will have weight, so the existence of feedforward insures that there is that potential, waiting to enter the next step in the process.

There are two main connections between feedforward/tacit knowing and people and machines. One is that the flexibility felt to exist in computer operation suggests that there is feedforward in the machine. That is, there is more in a machine than its designers were consciously placing there. (This is illustrated by the people who designed a computer that would perform addition, but who did not have the concept of multiplication. Yet, the capacity for multiplication was placed in the machine, and could be defined if the proper questions were put to the machine.) Therefore, the machine has tacit knowing that can be made explicit.

In a different dimension, computers in the mode of Information Systems for Vocational Decisions may enable people to bring more closely together tacit knowing and (explicit) knowing. In other words, *knowing* is an area or aspect of humanity where machines may contribute to the building of a receiver that does not exist at this time. This receiver will be able to pick up or define what feedforward only *feels* now. What is explicit can be interacted with by people and/or used by them in their further interactions with their environment, interactions that serve to define humankind.

The computer can be 1) both a feedforward and an undefined knowable thing, and 2) a means for people to feedforward, make the tacit explicit, and therefore define.

CAN A MACHINE CREATE A PERSON?

Robert W. White (1963) has spoken of growth in people as a process whereby the energy of the human organism moves toward constructing a stable, objective, real world on the basis of action. This description suggests that people can be defined by what they do. A computer, a machine, can be a target for some of that energy, just as can any other part of the environment. To the extent that people interact with a computer, they can be defined by that interaction. The fact that there is a computer in the environment, then, means that people will be created (defined) by that machine to the extent that they interact with it.

In another dimension the machine may also create because it will enable people to define their tacit knowing about creation, especially as that creation pertains to their own cognition-perception. There may be a singular quality to a computer such that it is a receiver for knowings that are at present unknowns—or that it has the potential for either becoming such or for making people such.

People are faced with the perplexing problems of relating knowledge to activity, of relating tacit knowledge to knowledge, and of relating unknown to tacit knowledge. We have our symbols for looking at knowledge, but however clever people are at developing language, language never matches experience. As Koestler reflects, we are symbol-wise but also symbol foolish. The computer, by its existence and by its *singular* existence, may be able to assist people in the creation of persons who can do this relating and get a perspective on their wise and foolish symbols—as it (and people in conjunction with it) works to create a receiver to bring into being the life of the mind that is now unknown.

Creation, growth, defining of a person, intrinsic learning, feedforward—such concepts ring with *education*: they are its end, and they the means to that end. They are the process of joining the life of the mind and the life of the world, the goal and the way for education. If a machine can, as we have argued, create a person, and the creation of people in the very broadest sense is the *raison d'etre* for education, what should that formal education be like? What should be the structure so that it is an agent for creating? Can formal education aspire to those delicious moments when a person is at one with the universe in the act of creating? How?

EDUCATION AND THE IMITATION OF CREATION

"I can't explain *myself*, I'm afraid, sir,
because I'm not myself, you see."

"I don't see," said the Caterpillar.

Lewis Carroll
Alice's Adventures in Wonderland

When we speak about education we must speak in terms of the learning process. The requirements of the learning process should be met by the educational structure. The learning process is an endless series of becomings; a move from the inside out, not from the outside in; a growing awareness of self; the move towards approaching the environment self-knowledgably to draw upon it to meet the needs of the self. Add to these happenings the heightened awareness and the moment of a subject revealing itself, and we have the vital signs of creating. What makes moments creating moments for man is the awarenss of self—again, the fusion of the life of the mind and the life of the world.

Our assumption is that the individual is the root and means and goal for the learning process, and for any system that seeks to serve it. Why learn? Rogers (1961) has asserted that there is a tendency existing in every individual to become its potentialities, and that it awaits only the proper conditions to be released and expressed. He sees the motivation for creativity as an individual's move to form new relationships with the environment in order to be itself. The most important question for individuals, then, is how they relate to the *world*. The essential resource for trying to answer this question is the people themselves.

Virginia Axline (1964) in the account of the remarkable growth of a child through psychotherapy, notes that "No one ever really knows as much about any human being's inner world as does the individual himself; that responsible freedom grows and develops from inside the person." Dibs, a little boy, gropes his way through his mixed-up feelings and slowly begins to see that he is capable of a great range of feeling and behavior. He could love and hate, forgive and despise, be real. In this case the goal was the child's self-knowledge and the resource for working towards that goal was the child.

What about means? When we speak of means we are talking of an imitation of creation. There are two important aspects of means for this learning—a learning we can now call self-creation. One is that we must start with individuals as they are. John Holt (1964) vividly referred to that starting point this way: "To rescue a man lost in the woods you must get to where he is." He recognizes that children have a style of learning that fits their condition and which they will use naturally unless forced to give up their style. Schools should be a place where children can use their style. A second aspect is what Tiedeman and Field (see Dudley and Tiedeman) have termed "purposeful action:" a "process of comparing the existing with the desired, of planning to secure the desired, and of acting contingently upon that plan . . . " This is personal goal-setting, and we use it in the sense that the goals are those of personal knowledge, self-awareness. Individuals move towards developing criteria for what is relevant to them about themselves.

What part can a machine play in the process? A machine that can help to make the tacit explicit, that can bring before people information about themselves in order that they can make decisions based upon this information, that can call upon what unknowns are within an individual; this kind of machine is essential for being an agent in the self-creating process. In other words, it seems possible to construct a machine that is consistent with the goals of education as outlined, and with, therefore, the imitation of creation.

But, we do not seek the ultimate machine to aid in the educational process. We do not endorse any one kind of machine. Such things are not representative of our purpose in this chapter. Although we seek ways in which machines can be employed as agents in the imitation of creation, our central concern with machines is with their heuristic value. The machine is a metaphor for the environment. The problem for education is not to develop a super-creating machine. It is rather to interact with the environment in a creating way. This way may involve computers as they exist today, or as they exist in somebody's or some machine's feedforward, or in ways that have not entered any feedforwards yet. But what kinds of machines, if any, are to be involved is not so important as what kind of an outlook is held about how people learn, how they interact with the environment, how people define themselves.

Is this chapter a machine? Does it serve to help in the construction of a receiver for the tacit knowledge that is in the feedforward stage? Can a chapter create a person? When we start asking such questions we come to see that the machine, even in the abstract, is of tremendous education potential. For an essential part of learning and of creating is the development of questions (receivers), in order that people can go out looking for what previously did not exist—because no one was looking for it. The exciting, stimulating quality of machines is that they are a means of self-knowing both in the abstract and potentially (the writer feels this moving from his feedforward into knowledge) in the concrete reality.

Yes, a machine can create a person. But let us rephrase the question now and ask the following: Can a person create a person? We will give people machines to use to solve this problem if they wish—in fact, all of the environment, including self-knowledge is a permissible resource. How then will people move to join the life of the mind and the life of the world? For that joining, however it is done, has been the subject of this chapter.

Appendix A

ACKNOWLEDGEMENTS

The design and construction of the prototypic Information System for Vocational Decisions was not an individual effort. The following persons participated in both the design and construction of the System in their noted roles:

In liaison through the United States Office of Education

Norman Boyan, Acting Associate Commissioner, Bureau of Research, Office of Education (1969)

R. Louis Bright, Associate Commissioner of Research, Office of Education (through 1968)

Clay V. Brittain, Project Officer, Human Resources Branch, Division of Adult and Vocational Research

David E. Bushnell, Director, Division of Comprehensive and Vocational Education Research

Lawrence G. Gobel, Acting Branch Director, Basic Studies Branch, Division of Comprehensive and Vocational Education Research (1968-69)

Eunice Jones, Project Officer, Human Resources Branch, Division of Adult and Vocational Research (through November, 1966)

Richard B. Otte, Project Officer, Human Resources Branch, Division of Adult and Vocational Research (Dec. 1966-Oct. 1967)

David Pollin, Deputy Associate U.S. Commisioner (Research)

Alice Y. Scates, Branch Director, Basic Studies Branch, Division of Comprehensive and Vocational Education Research (through Dec. 1968)
Senior Program Associate, Program Planning and Evaluation, Bureau of Research

Judith D. Weinstein, Project Officer, Basic Studies Branch, Division of Comprehensive and Vocational Education Research (1969)

In liaison, Division of Vocational Education, Department of Education, Commonwealth of Massachusetts

Walter Markham, Director of Bureau of Vocational Education

John P. Morine, Member of Advisory Committee; and Senior Supervisor, Occupational Information and Vocational Guidance

In liaison through the Office of Dean, Harvard Graduate School of Education

Jane Batchelder, Administrative Assistant in charge of Personnel (through 1968)

Herman F. Eschenbacher, Member, *ex officio*, of Advisory Committee (resigned June, 1967), Librarian; and Lecturer in Education

Dorothy A. Johnson, Administrative Assistant in the Office of the Dean

Edward G. Kaelber, Associate Dean (resigned February, 1968)

Paul A. Perry, Assistant Dean

Gertrude Rogers, Administrative Assistant in charge of Personnel

Richard R. Rowe, Associate Dean (1968-69)

Theodore R. Sizer, Member, *ex officio*, Executive Committee, and Dean

Richard C. Wheeler, Associate Director of Placement

Ronald Wormser, Assistant to the Dean for Administration

In liaison through the New England School Development Council—New England Education Data Systems

Raimond Bowles, Director of Finance, NESDEC

Richard Goodman, Executive Secretary, NESDEC-NEEDS; Chairman, Board of Directors, NEEDS (through summer 1969)

Hilton C. Holland, Chairman, Executive Committee, NESDEC

Robert Ireland, Executive Secretary, NESDEC (summer 1969)

Eugene Park, Director of School Services, NEEDS

Michael Wilson, Executive Officer, NESDEC-NEEDS (resigned 1969)

In liaison, Western Metropolitan Boston Regional Opportunity Council (WEMBROC)

Joseph H. McPherson, Manpower Director

In liaison, Technical Institutes

Paul Berwick, Admissions and Counseling, Springfield (Massachusetts) Technical Community College

Richard Borowski, Counseling Center, Milwaukee Technical Institute

John Bugbee, Biomedical Technical Instruction, Springfield (Massachusetts) Technical Community College

Jimmy Hunter, Paul Quinn College (Waco, Texas)

Elmer Kuntz, James Connally Technical Institute (Waco, Texas)

Thomas Penwitz, Computer Area, Milwaukee Technical Institute

Dennis Redovich, Placement Center, Milwaukee Technical Institute

Alfred St. Onge, Computer Systems, Springfield (Massachusetts) Technical Community College

Theodore Talbot, Paul Quinn College (Waco, Texas)

Advisory Committee

+*E. Gil Boyer (resigned April, 1966), Administrator, NEEDS (June, 1963-June 1966)

Charles T. W. Curle, Professor of Education and Development, Harvard Graduate School of Education

+*Russell G. Davis, Professor of Education and Development; Research Associate in Center for Studies in Education and Development, Harvard Graduate School of Education

Howard W. Dillon (appointed June, 1967), Librarian, Harvard Graduate School of Education

+*Richard M. Durstine, Research Associate in Center for Studies in Education and Development; Lecturer in Education, Harvard Graduate School of Education

+*Allan B. Ellis, Director, Center for Educational Software Development, NESDEC; Lecturer in Education, Harvard Graduate School of Education

Herman F. Eschenbacher (resigned June, 1967), Librarian, Harvard Graduate School of Education (July, 1965-July, 1967)

+*Wallace J. Fletcher, Research Associate, Harvard Graduate School of Education; President, Western Metropolitan Boston Regional Opportunity Council, Inc.

Thomas E. Kurtz (appointed June, 1967), Director, Kiewit Computation Center, Dartmouth College

+*Edward Landy, Assistant Superintendent of the Newton Public School System and Director of Pupil Personnel Services and Special Education, Newton Public School Department

Emmanuel G. Mesthene, Executive Director, University Program on Technology and Society, Harvard University

John D. Morine, Senior Supervisor, Occupational Information and Vocational Guidance, Division of Vocational Education, Department of Education, Commonwealth of Massachusetts

+*Robert P. O'Hara, Executive Director, Information System for Vocational Decisions

* Theodore R. Sizer, *ex officio*; Dean, Harvard Graduate School of Education

+*David V. Tiedeman, Chairman; Professor of Education, Harvard Graduate School of Education; Chairman, Executive Committee, Information System for Vocational Decisions

+*Michael J. Wilson, Executive Officer, New England Education Data Systems (resigned 1969)

Norman Zachary (resigned April, 1967), Director, Harvard Computing Center

+ Principal Investigator
* Member of Executive Committee

Research Associates

David K. Archibald (October, 1968-July, 1969)

Robert D. Brown (Sept., 1968-July, 1969)

Duncan F. Circle (resigned June, 1968)

David B. Clemens (resigned June, 1967)

Thomas E. Hutchinson (December, 1968-July, 1969)

Arthur M. Kroll (resigned June, 1967)

Lawrence Lerer (resigned December, 1968)

Noel F. McGinn (resigned January, 1967)

Terence J. O'Mahoney (December, 1968-July, 1969)

Stephen Purcell (summer, 1967)

Eugene H. Wilson (resigned October, 1968)

Systems Specialists

David Brewster (resigned June, 1969)

Roy E. Norris, Jr.

Heather Scott

Graham Smith (November, 1968-February, 1969)

Ann W. Taylor

Programmers

Toby Boyd (resigned October, 1968)

Arlene Scherer (resigned April, 1969)

Computer Operators

M. Sue Kaiser   Marjorie Madoff

Principals (Newton School Department)

Robert Frost   Muriel L. Lundy

Richard W. Mechem

Counselors (Newton School Department)

James Hartman   Dorothy Kunberger

James McDade   Archibald Stark

Myra Trachtenberg

Script Writers

Jon H. Abrahamson (summer, 1967)

Margaret Addis (summer, 1967)

Gerald Bazer (summer, (1967)

Joseph Clancy (summer, 1967)

Neil Curran (summer, 1967)

Hope Danielson (summer, 1967)

Sara Eddy (summer, 1967)

Gail Gassen (summer, 1967)

James Hartman (summer, 1967)

Robert W. Hayes (summer, 1967)

Patricia Kelley (summer, 1967)

Frank Lambert (summer, 1967)

Cecile P. LeClair (summer, 1967)

Paul H. Linscott (summer, 1967)

Peter A. Mackie (summer, 1967)

Dorothy A. Mahoney (summer, 1967)

James M. McGovern (summer, 1967)

Linda McLean (summer, 1967)

Carolyn Mellor (summer, 1967)

Emory Miller (summer, 1968)

William H. Moore, Jr. (summer, 1967)

Vivian Parker (summer, 1967)

Bruce Pelton (summer, 1967)

Catherine Psyhogios (summer, 1967)

Robert M. Rosenblatt (summer, 1967)

Howard Schofield (summer, 1967)

Anne Stamas (summer, 1967)

Archibald Stark (summer, 1967)

Nancy Swidler (summer, 1967 and 1968)

Armine D. Thomason (summer, 1967)

Joseph M. Utka (summer, 1967)

Audio Visual Specialist

Elaine Fisher (May, 1968-July, 1969)

Administrative Assistants and Associate Editors

Sheila Ary (winter, 1978)

Sara S. Booth (resigned April, 1969)

Sheila Leahy (April, 1969-August, 1969)

Nona D. Strauss (resigned August, 1969)

Research Assistants and Technicians

Robert Aylmer, Jr.

Susan Baldwin (October, 1967-March, 1968)

Nancy Blackmun (summer, 1966)

Christopher Davis (summer, 1967)

Lawrence Dougherty (September, 1967-September, 1968)

Gordon A. Dudley (resigned August, 1967)

Patcick F. Ferrone (summer, 1966)

Lynne Fitzhugh (resigned 1968)

Myra T. Gannaway

Charles E. Gunnoe

Thomas E. Hutchinson (appointed Research Associate, December, 1968)

Diana J. Kronstadt (resigned July, 1968)

Sheila Leahy

Priscilla A. Little

Sandra J. Morse (summer, 1966)

Terence J. O'Mahoney (appointed Research Associate, December, 1968)

Margeret E. Pincus (resigned May, 1968)

Dana E. Quitslund (resigned December, 1968)

Charles Roehrig (May, 1968-September, 1968)

Richard Roman

Susan Roman (resigned June, 1969)

Stanley A. Schainker (resigned September, 1967)

Johanna Seltzer (resigned June, 1967)

Herbert Simons

Arnold Smith (February, 1968-June, 1968)

Dorothy S. Swithenbank (resigned September, 1968)

Thomas E. Swithenbank (resigned September, 1968)

Elizabeth Truesdell

Joe Weissman (June, 1968-August, 1968)

Esther Wiedman (resigned September, 1968)

Charles S. Wetherell (resigned August, 1967)

Laurence Wolff (resigned October, 1967)

Patricia Yee

Barbara Zurer (resigned May, 1967)

Communications Technician

Richard F. Topping

Secretaries

Patricia Capen (summer, 1968)

Martha Drake

Dorothy Julia Emerson (resigned June, 1968)

Karen Guillette (resigned September, 1967)

Marietta Haley

Susan Hartman

Jacqueline Hargrove (resigned July, 1967)

Luann Heidan (winter, 1978)

Nadia Hurt (resigned February, 1967)

Linda LeBlanc

Alvis Martinez

Jean MacQuiddy (resigned April, 1967)

Wendy Mahon (resigned June, 1968)

Felice A. Merritt (resigned September, 1967)

Susan Morrison

Doborah Richardson

Wendy Simpson

Nona D. Strauss

Helen E. Topping

Clerks

Jayne Lyons (resigned June, 1967)

Annette B. Miller (resigned June, 1968)

Mary A. O'Doherty (resigned June, 1967)

Keypunch Operator

Dorothy Boudreau (September, 1968-   )

Couriers

James P. Dean (resigned June, 1968)

Dennis Horger (September, 1968-June, 1969)

Robert Sullivan (summer, 1968,1969)

Consultants

Frank L. Field, University of California at Santa Barbara (July, 1968)

Warren Gribbons, Regis College (summer, 1965)

Chris Kehas, Claremont Graduate School (summer, 1967)

Paul Lohnes, Project TALENT (summer and fall, 1967)

Esther Matthews, University of Oregon (summer, 1967)

Frank J. Minor (time contributed by International Business Machines Corp., Inc.)

Calvin Mooers, Rockford Research Institute, Inc. (summer and fall, 1966)

George D. Pasquella, Film Consultant (May, 1968)

Stanley Segal, Teachers College, Columbia University (summer, 1967)

Sub-Contractors

Abt Associates (spring, 1967)

Computer Associates (spring and summer, 1967)

Visiting Researchers

Fran Archambault, University of Connecticut

Roy Forbes, General Learning Corporation

John McManus, University of Connecticut

William Mittlestadt, Eastman Kodak Co.

Gary Stapleford, Sanders Associates

Selwyn Taylor, Sanders Associates

Keith Whitmore, Eastman Kodak Co.

Appendix B

ISVD REPORTS AND CONTEXT

The project also gave rise to the following reports which can be pursued as desired in expansion of the general argument of this book:

TECHNICAL MEMORANDA

No. 1—"The Computer and Career Decisions" by Allan B. Ellis and Charles S. Wetherell.

No. 2—"Forecasting for Computer Aided Career Decisions: Survey of Methodology" by Russell G. Davis.

No. 3—"Level of Aspiration and Models Applicable to the Problem of Choice of Career" by Thomas E. Huchinson.

PROJECT REPORTS

No. 1—"The Organization and Intention of a Proposed Data and Educational System for Vocational Decision-Making" by David V. Tiedeman.

No. 2—"An Information System for Vocational Decisions (ISVD): Cultivating the Possibility for Career through Operations" by David V. Tiedeman.

No. 3—"A Theoretical Foundation for the Use of Occupational Information in Guidance" by Robert P. O'Hara.

No. 4—"Suggestions for Treatment of Information about Occupations" by Richard M. Durstine.

No. 5—"Self Esteem Because of Collegiate Admission and Education" by David V. Tiedeman.

No. 6—"Forecasting for Computer Aided Decisions: Prospects and Procedures" by Richard M. Durstine.

No. 19—"Can a Machine Admit an Applicant to Continuing Education?" by David V. Tiedeman.

No. 20—"On the Concept of Purpose" by Frank L. Field of the University of California at Stanta Barbara.

No. 21—"A Quasi-Annotated Sourcelist for Occupational Forecasting" by Patricia Yee.

Several doctoral dissertations and projects were completed because of the Information System for Vocational Decisions as well. The ones which are relevant to the philosophy and technology of the ISVD are:

Aylmer, Robert C., Jr. *A Preliminary Investigation of Computer Involvement in Vocational Decision-Making.* Cambridge, MA: Harvard Graduate School of Education, 1970. (Unpublished doctoral dissertation)

Brown, Roger D. *The Administration of a Self-Evaluation of the Guidance Program at the Warren Junior High School in the Newton, Massachusetts Public Schools.* Cambridge, MA: Harvard Graduate School of Education, 1969. (Unpublished doctoral project report)

Carhart, Richard L. *Death-angst: A Synthesis in Developmental Perspective.* DeKalb, IL: Northern Illinois University, 1977. (Unpublished doctoral dissertation)

Carle, Richard F. *The Process of Decision Concerning Entry Into the Field of Education: A Study of Education-Industry Interaction.* Cambridge, MA: Harvard Graduate School of Education, 1969. (Unpublished doctoral project report)

Cathcart, Lee Perry. *The Collaboration of Theories in Elementary School Guidance.* Cambridge, MA: Harvard Graduate School of Education, 1970. (Unpublished doctoral dissertation)

Circle, Duncan F. *The Organization and Establishment, Through the Position of Coordinator, of a System-Wide Vocational Placement Service in the Newton, Massachusetts, Public Schools.* Cambridge, MA: Harvard Graduate School of Education, 1968. (Unpublished doctoral project report)

Circle, Duncan F.; Clemens, David B.; Kroll, Arthur M.; and Overholdt, Dorothea C. *The Career Information Service: A Guide to Its Development and Use.* Newton, MA: Newton Public Schools, 1968.

Clemens, David B. *The Introduction, Organization, and Development of a Follow-up Program in the Newton Public Schools Using Data Processing Procedures.* Cambridge, MA: Harvard Graduate School of Education, 1966. (Unpublished doctoral project report)

deGregoris, Vincent. *An Investigation of Career Development in Graduate Theological Students: An Analysis of Retrospective Career Reports with Implications for Guidance in Admissions and Education.* Cambridge, MA: Harvard Graduate School of Education, 1971. (Unpublished doctoral dissertation)

Dudley, Gordon A. *Aspects of Imagination in the Learning Process.* Cambridge, MA: Harvard Graduate School of Education, 1971. (Unpublished doctoral dissertation)

Dykeman, Bruce F. *The Effectiveness of a Career Education Program in Developing the Vocational Maturity of Potential Dropouts.* DeKalb, IL: Northern Illinois University, 1977. (Unpublished doctoral dissertation)

Elenz-Martin, Patricia. *A Study of the Pre-occupational Effects of the Resident Assistant Experience on Career Decision Making During the College Years.* DeKalb, IL: Northern Illinois University, 1977. (Unpublished doctoral dissertation)

Field, Frank L. *An Investigation of Decision-Making in an Education-Vocational Context with Implications for Guidance.* Cambridge, MA: Harvard Graduate School of Education, 1964. (Unpublished doctoral dissertation)

Firth, John L. *Retirement as Transition: A Study of the Meanings of Post-Vocational Activities of Retired Males.* Cambridge, MA: Harvard Graduate School of Education, 1969. (Unpublished doctoral dissertation)

Gannaway, Myra R. *A Blueprint for Species-Constructive Education: A Unifying Approach.* Cambridge, MA: Harvard Graduate School of Education, 1973. (Unpublished doctoral dissertation)

Geist, Richard A. *Children and Psychology in Crisis: A Study in Psychological Consultation to Junior High School Children.* Cambridge, MA: Harvard Graduate School of Education, 1970. (Unpublished doctoral dissertation)

Gillen, W. King. *The Implementation and Evaluation of a Computer-Based Career Information System.* Cambridge, MA: Harvard Graduate School of Education, 1968. (Unpublished doctoral project report)

Goodman, Natalie C. *Leisure, Work, and the Use of Time: A Study of Adult Style of Time Utilization, Childhood Determinants and Vocational Implications.* Cambridge, MA: Harvard Graduate School of Education, 1969. (Unpublished doctoral dissertation)

Hutchinson, Thomas E. *Level of Aspiration and Statistical Models Applicable to the Problem of Refining Choice Bases for Career Development: Logic with Implications.* Cambridge, MA: Harvard Graduate School of Education, 1969. (Unpublished doctoral dissertation)

Jordan, John Q. *Computer Concepts: A Proposal for Training Teachers.* Cambridge, MA: Harvard Graduate School of Education, 1970. (Unpublished doctoral dissertation)

Katz, Martin R. *The Development and Evaluation of a Guidance Text for Eighth or Ninth Grade.* Cambridge, MA: Harvard Graduate School of Education, 1960. (Unpublished doctoral dissertation)

Kehas, Chris D. *An Analysis of Self Concept Theory and the Application of the Findings to a Study of Achievement in School.* Cambridge, MA: Harvard Graduate School of Education, 1964. (Unpublished doctoral dissertation)

Kroll, Arthur M. *Facilitation of Student Self-Evaluation in Career Development Through Improvements in the Information Service of the Guidance Program in the Newton, Massachusetts, Public Schools.* Cambridge, MA: Harvard Graduate School of Education, 1966. (Unpublished doctoral project report)

Kubistant, Thomas M. *A Synthesis of the Aloneness/Loneliness Phenomenon: A Counseling Perspective.* DeKalb, IL: Northern Illinois University, 1977. (Unpublished doctoral dissertation)

Landy, Stephen. *The Known and the Measured: A Consideration of Certain Implicit Assumptions in Testing in the Light of Some Recent Additions to the Theory of Knowledge.* Cambridge, MA: Harvard Graduate School of Education, 1970. (Unpublished qualifying paper)

Lee, Robert R. *Implementing a Cooperative Work-Study Program for High School Educable Mentally-Retarded Students Through a Title III Supplementary Education Center.* Cambridge, MA: Harvard Graduate School of Education, 1970. (Unpublished doctoral project report)

Lerer, Lawrence. *Coordinating Efforts for the Development and Implementation of a Cooperative Work-Study Program Involving the Newton Public Schools, Newton City Hall, Newton Community Action, Inc., and the Industrial Community.* Cambridge, MA: Harvard School of Education, 1967. (Unpublished doctoral project report)

Lowy, Louis. *Clarification of Self and Role Perceptions in Social Work Students During Training: A Study of Incorporation of a Professional Role.* Cambridge, MA: Harvard Graduate School of Education, 1966. (Unpublished doctoral dissertation)

Marks, Sema. *A Course in Computer Simulation for High School Students.* Cambridge, MA: Harvard Graduate School of Education, 1970. (Unpublished doctoral dissertation)

Marsden, Gerald. *A Psychological Study of Working Boys.* Cambridge, MA: Harvard Graduate School of Education, 1967. (Unpublished doctoral dissertation)

Matthews, Esther E. *The Marriage-Career Conflict in the Career Development of Girls and Young Women.* Cambridge, MA: Harvard Graduate School of Education, 1960. (Unpublished doctoral dissertation)

Miller-Tiedeman, Anna. *A Structural Exploration of a Career Sense of the Future.* Athens, OH: Ohio University, 1973. (Unpublished doctoral dissertation)

Morley, Eileen D. *Human Services in Complex Work Organizations: A Study of the Patterning of Proadaptive Human Services in Industrial Work-Systems, and the Relation of the Presence of Such Services to Organizational Characteristics.* Cambridge, MA: Harvard Graduate School of Education, 1971. (Unpublished doctoral dissertation)

Murphy, William F. *Discovery Strategies for Process Goals of Education: The Problem of Behavioral Specification.* Cambridge, MA: Harvard Graduate School of Education, 1968. (Unpublished qualifying paper)

Ng, Pedro Pak-tao. *A Causal Approach to the Study of Satisfaction in the Academic Profession.* Cambridge, MA: Harvard Graduate School of Education, 1971. (Unpublished doctoral dissertation)

O'Hara, Robert P. *On the Importance of the Self Concept to a General Theory of Occupational Choice.* Cambridge, MA: Harvard Graduate School of Education, 1957. (Unpublished qualifying paper)

O'Hara, Robert P. *A Cross Sectional Study of Growth in the Relationship of Self Ratings and Test Scores.* Cambridge, MA: Harvard Graduate School of Education, 1958. (Unpublished doctoral dissertation)

O'Mahoney, Terrence J. *Self Development Processes: A Model and an Heuristic Procedure for Investigating Aspects of These Processes.* Leeds, England: University of Leeds, 1968. (Unpublished doctoral dissertation)

Pandit, Jiwan Lal. *Self Consistency as a Factor in Occupational Aspiration of Male High School Seniors and Juniors.* Cambridge, MA: Harvard Graduate School of Education, 1958. (Unpublished doctoral dissertation)

Parker, L. Allen. *Interactive Networks for Innovational Champions: A Mechanism for Decentralized Educational Change.* Cambridge, MA: Harvard Graduate School of Education, 1971. (Unpublished doctoral dissertation)

Payzant, Thomas W. *Planning for Meeting the Changing Vocational and Technical Education Needs of a City School System.* Cambridge, MA: Harvard Graduate School of Education, 1968. (Unpublished doctoral dissertation)

Pillinger, Barbara B. *An Exploration of Choice in a Voluntary College Physical Education Program.* Cambridge, MA: Harvard Graduate School of Education, 1972. (Unpublished doctoral dissertation)

Powell, Douglas Hagen. *Family Atmosphere and Other Childhood Patterns as Precursors of Career Interests.* Cambridge, MA: Harvard Graduate School of Education, 1959. (Unpublished doctoral dissertation)

Ramsey, Robert R., Jr. *A Study of Cultural Influence on Academic Performance in College and Law School.* Cambridge, MA: Harvard Graduate School of Education, 1959. (Unpublished doctoral dissertation)

Roman, Richard A. *Developing and Implementing Computer-Based Instructional Materials.* Cambridge, MA: Harvard Graduate School of Education, 1969. (Unpublished doctoral project report)

Rutherford, Harry B. *Cultivating Purposeful Action at Coolidge Senior High School Through a Program of Individual Counseling.* Cambridge, MA: Harvard Graduate School of Education, 1969. (Unpublished doctoral project report)

Santonicola, Anthony T. *Identity, Decision Making and Time Perspective in Late Adolescence.* Cambridge, MA: Harvard Graduate School of Education, 1970. (Unpublished doctoral dissertation)

Scheffler, Rosalin Z. *From Five to Six: A Longitudinal Study of Psychodynamic Change.* Cambridge, MA: Harvard Graduate School of Education, 1971. (Unpublished doctoral dissertation)

Shea, Paul D. *Parental Influence on College Planning by Boys and Girls of High Ability During the Sixth to the Ninth Grades.* Cambridge, MA: Harvard Graduate School of Education, 1963. (Unpublished doctoral dissertation)

Smith, S. Corbin. *Understanding Educational and Individual Psychological Development With Particular Concern for Issues of Freedom and Control.* Cambridge, MA: Harvard Graduate School of Education, 1971. (Unpublished qualifying paper)

Warren, William H. *Administrative Functions in Facilitating a Systems Approach to General Education and Guidance in a College.* Cambridge, MA: Harvard Graduate School of Education, 1967. (Unpublished doctoral project report)

Werthemier, Patricia A. *Improving School Climate: Building Team Relationships.* Cambridge, MA: Harvard Graduate School of Education, 1970. (Unpublished doctoral project report)

Williamson, John N. *The Inquiring School: A Study of Educational Self-Renewal.* Cambridge, MA: Harvard Graduate School of Education, 1971. (Unpublished doctoral dissertation)

Wilson, Eugene H. *A Critical Review of Theory and Research on the Teaching of Decision-Making During Adolescence and Young Adulthood.* Cambridge, MA: Harvard Graduate School of Education, 1966. (unpublished qualifying paper)

Wilson, Eugene H. *The Development and Pilot Testing of a System for the Teaching of Decision-Making.* Cambridge, MA: Harvard Graduate School of Education, 1971. (Unpublished doctoral dissertation)

Worthen, John E. *The Development and Implementation of a Program of Guidance Through the Position of Assistant Director and Instructor in the Harvard-Lexington Summer School.* Cambridge, MA: Harvard Graduate School of Education, 1964. (Unpublished doctoral project report)

Appendix C

CATEGORIES OF INFORMATION FROM THE 850 TITLES FILE AND FROM THE D.O.T. SUPPLEMENT

Category	In 850 Titles File	In D.O.T. Supplement
1. Occupational title	yes	yes
2. Alternate titles	up to five	
3. Entry occupations	up to four	
4. Higher occupations	up to four	
5. Industries where found	up to four	one only
6. Brief verbal description	yes	
7. Worker trait sector (from D.O.T.)	yes	yes
8. Aptitudes: General intelligence	five levels	five levels
9. Aptitudes: Verbal ability	five levels	five levels
10. Aptitudes: Numerical ability	five levels	five levels
11. Aptitudes: Spatial perception	five levels	five levels
12. Aptitudes: Form perception	five levels	five levels
13. Aptitudes: Clerical perception	five levels	five levels
14. Aptitudes: Motor Coordination	five levels	five levels

15. Aptitudes: Finger dexterity	five levels	five levels
16. Aptitudes: Manual dexterity	five levels	five levels
17. Aptitudes: Eye-Hand-Foot coordination	five levels	five levels
18. Aptitudes: Color discrimination	five levels	five levels
19. Interest preferences	up to three	
20. Occupational situations	up to three	up to five
21. Strength required	five levels	five levels
22. Physical demands	up to five	up to five
23. Required high school courses	36 possibilities	
24. Salaries and wages	three levels	
25. Required academic ability	four levels	
26. Required mechanical ability	four levels	
27. Required social intelligence	four levels	
28. Required clerical ability	four levels	
29. Required musical ability	four levels	
30. Required artistic ability	four levels	
31. Required physical ability	four levels	
32. Most common prior activity	up to two	
33. On-the-job training	eight levels	See item 63

34. Formal education required	eight levels	See item 62
35. Formal education preferred	eight levels	See item 62
36. Recommended school courses	up to four	
37. Short training courses	up to two	
38. Distribution of sexes	five levels	
39. Mininum age	yes	
40. License requirement	yes	
41. Union membership	yes	
42. Working conditions	up to six	up to six
43. Place of work (indoor, outdoor)	yes	yes
44. Weekend work	three levels	
45. Hours of work	three levels	
46. Requirements for travel	three levels	
47. Seasonality	yes	
48. Basis of income	four levels	
49. Incentives and fringe benefits	up to four	
50. Opportunities for promotion	four levels	
51. Paths for promotion	up to two	
52. Opportunities for mobility	four levels	
53. Possibility of self-employment	yes	
54. Growth rate of occupation	four levels	
55. Demand for workers	five levels	

56. Trend of wages	three levels	
57. Worker functions— data		ten levels
58. Worker functions— people		nine levels
59. Worker functions— things		eleven levels
60. Work fields		up to two
61. D.O.T. number	yes	old and new
62. General educational development	See items 34,35	six levels
63. Specific vocational preparation	See item 33	nine levels
64. Materials, products, subject matter		up to two

NOTES:

There is some redundancy among the categories of the 850 Titles File that must be worked out in its use.

The two data files described here are merged into one for operation within the ISVD.

In all cases there is a possibility that "not applicable," "no information" or some similar null message can be coded as appropriate.

REFERENCES

Axline, Virginia Mae. **Dibs: in Search of Self.** Boston: Houghton Mifflin, 1964.

Bobrow, D. G. **A Question Answerer for Algebra Work Problems. Memo 45.** Cambridge, MA: Artificial Intelligence Project, MIT, 1963.

Boocock, Sarane. *The Life Career Game,* **Personnel and Guidance Journal,** 1967, 46, 328-334.

Bordin, Edward S.; Nachmann, Barbara; and Segal, Stanley J. *An Articulated Framework for Vocational Development,* **Journal of Counseling Psychology,** 1963, 10, 107-117.

Bronowski, Jacob. **The Identity of Man.** Garden City, NY: The Natural History Press, 1965.

Camus, Albert. **L'Envers et L'Endroit.** Paris: Gallimard, 1958.

Carroll, John B; and Ellis, Allan B. **Planning and Utilization of a Regional Data Bank for Educational Research Purposes.** Cambridge, MA: Harvard Graduate School of Education, Harvard University, 1965.

Clarke, Arthur C. **2001: A Space Odyssey.** (movie)

Coles, Robert. **Children of Crisis.** New York: Delta, 1967.

Cooley, William W.; and Lohnes, Paul. **Predicting Development of Young Adults.** Palo Alto, CA: American Institutes for Research, 1968.

Crites, John O. *Measurement of Vocational Maturity in Adolescence: 1. Attitude Test of the Vocational Development Inventory,* **Psychological Monographs: General and Applied,** 1965, 79, 1-36.

Crites, John O. **Vocational Psychology.** New York: McGraw-Hill, 1969.

Dudley, Gordon A. *Creativity and Career: A Discussion of the Role of Symbolic Processes of Ego Synthesis in the Psychology of Vocational Development.* Cambridge, MA: Harvard Graduate School of Education, 1966. (Unpublished qualifying paper)

Dudley, Gordon A., and Tiedeman, David V. **Career Development: Exploration and Commitment.** Muncie, IN: Accelerated Development, 1977.

Ellis, Allan B., and Wetherell, Charles S. **The Computer and Career Decision. Technical Memorandum No. 1.** Cambridge, MA: Information System for Vocational Decisions, Harvard Graduate School of Education, 1966.

Erikson, Erik H. *Identity and the Life Cycle.* **Psychological Issues,** 1959, 1, 1-171.

Field, Frank L. *An Investigation of Decision-Making in an Educational-Vocational Context with Implications for Guidance.* Cambridge, MA: Harvard Graduate School of Education, 1964. (Unpublished doctoral dissertation)

Field, Frank L. *Toward an Operational Goal for Guidance-in-Education: A Working Paper for Program Development.* Santa Barbara, CA: School of Education, University of California, 1964. (mimeo)

Field, Frank L. **On the Concept of Purpose. Project Report No. 20.** Cambridge, MA: Information System for Vocational Decisions, Harvard Graduate School of Education, 1969.

Fromm, Erich. **Man for Himself.** New York: Holt, Rhinehart, Winston, 1947.

Gannaway, Myra T. *Changing Perspectives in Education and Self-Correcting Thinking.* Cambridge, MA: Harvard Graduate School of Education, 1968. (Unpublished qualifying paper)

CAREER DEVELOPMENT

Ginzberg, Eli. **Career Guidance: Who Needs It, Who Can Improve It.** New York: McGraw-Hill, 1971.

Ginzberg, Eli; Ginsburg, Sol W.; Axelrad, Sidney; and Herma, John L. **Occupational Choice: An Approach to a General Theory.** New York: Columbia University Press, 1951.

Green, B. F.; Chomsky, C.; Laughery, K.; and Wolf, A. K. *Baseball: An Automatic Question-Answerer,* **Proceedings of the Western Joint Computer Conference,** 1961, 19, 219-224.

Gribbons, Warren D. *Determination of Progress in Educational and Vocational Planning in Adolescence.* Cambridge, MA: Harvard Graduate School of Education, 1959. (Unpublished doctoral dissertation)

Gross, Edward. *A Sociological Approach to the Analysis of Preparation for Work Life.* In Campbell, Robert E. (Ed.) **Guidance in Vocational Education: Guidelines for Research and Practice.** Columbus, OH: The Center for Vocational Education, the Ohio State University, 1966, pp. 50-60.

Hayward, P. R. **ELIZA Scriptwriter's Manual.** Cambridge, MA: Education Research Center, MIT, 1968.

Helm, C. E. **Simulation Models for Psychometric Theories.** Princeton, NJ: Princeton University, 1965.

Holland, John L. *A Theory of Vocational Choice,* **Journal of Counseling Psychology,** 1959, 6, 35-45.

Holland, John L. **The Psychology of Vocational Choice.** Waltham, MA: Blaisdell, 1966.

Holt, John. **How Children Fail.** New York: Dell, 1964.

Hummel, Thomas J.; Lichtenberg, James W.; and Shaffer, Warren F. *CLIENT 1: A Computer Program which Simulates Client Behavior in an Initial Interview.* **Journal of Counseling Psychology,** 1975, 22, 164-169.

Hutchinson, Thomas E. **Level of Aspiration and Models Applicable to the Problem of Choice of Career. Technical Memorandum No. 3.** Cambridge, MA: Information System for Vocational Decisions, Harvard Graduate School of Education, 1967.

Katz, Martin R. **A Computer-Assisted System of Interactive Guidance and Information to Improve Career Decision-Making in Junior Colleges. A Proposal to Carnegie Corporation of New York.** Princeton, NJ: Educational Testing Service, 1968.

Kehas, Chris D. *An Analysis of Self-Concept Theory and the Application of the Findings to a Study of Achievement in School.* Cambridge, MA: Harvard Graduate School of Education, 1964. (Unpublished doctroal dissertation)

Koestler, Arthur. **The Act of Creation.** New York: Dell, 1964.

Landy, Stephen. *The Known and the Measured: A Consideration of Certain Implicit Assumptions in Testing in the Light of Some Recent Additions to the Theory of Knowledge.* Cambridge, MA: Harvard Graduate School of Education, 1968. (Unpublished qualifying paper)

Marland, S. P., Jr. **Career Education Now.** Bathesda, MD 20014: ERIC Document Reproduction Service, Leasco Information Products (LIPCO), 4827 Rugby Avenue, 1971. (Order ED 048 480.)

Marland, S. P., Jr. **Career Education and Equality of Opportunity.** Bathesda, MD 20014: ERIC Document Reproduction Service, Leasco Information Products (LIPCO), 4827 Rugby Avenue, 1973. (Order ED 080 850.)

Maslow, Abraham. *Self Actualization and Beyond.* 1965. (mimeo)

Matthews, Esther. *The Marriage-Career Conflict in the Career of Girls and Young Women.* Cambridge, MA: Harvard Graduate School of Education, 1960. (Unpublished doctoral dissertation)

CAREER DEVELOPMENT

McKeon, Editor. **The Works of Aristotle.** New York: Random House, 1947.

Miller, Tiedeman, Anna; and Tiedeman, David V. **Career Development: "I" Power.** Schenectady, NY: Character Research Press, 1978. (in press)

Mooers, Calvin. *TRAC, A Test Handling Language,* **Proceedings of the ACM, 20th National Conference,** 1965, 229-246.

Morley, Eileen; and Tiedeman, David V. *Confidence: Key to Vocational Competence.* **Metals Review,** 1966, 2, 19-20.

Oates, W.; and O'Neill, E., Jr. (Ed.) **The Complete Greek Drama.** 1. New York: Random House, 1938.

O'Hara, Robert P. *A Cross-Sectional Study of Growth in the Relationship of Self Ratings and Test Scores.* Cambridge, MA: Harvard Graduate School of Education, 1958. (Unpublished doctoral dissertation)

O'Mahoney, Terence J. *Self Development Processes: A Model and An Heuristic Procedure for Investigating Aspects of These Processes.* Leeds, England: University of Leeds, 1968. (Unpublished doctoral dissertation)

Peatling, John H.; and Tiedeman, David V. **Career Development: Designing Self.** Muncie, IN: Accelerated Development, 1977.

Polanyi, Michael. **The Study of Man.** Chicago: University of Chicago Press, 1959.

Polanyi, Michael. **The Tacit Dimension.** Garden City: Doubleday, 1966.

Richards, Ivor A. **Speculative Instruments.** New York: Harcourt, Brace, and World, 1955.

Richards, Ivor A. *The Secret of Feedforward.* **Saturday Review.** February 3, 1968, pp. 14-17.

Roe, Anne. **The Psychology of Occupations.** New York: Harper and Row, 1956.

Rogers, Carl R. **On Becoming a Person.** Boston: Houghton Mifflin, 1961.

Rulon, Phillip J.; Tiedeman, David V.; Tatsuoka, Maurice M.; and Langmuir, Charles R. **Multivarite Statistics for Personnel Classification.** New York: John Wiley, 1967.

Schwab, Joseph. **The Teaching of Science as Enquiry.** Cambridge, MA: Harvard University Press, 1962.

Simmons, R. F. *Synthex: Toward Computer Synthesis of Human Language Behavior.* In H. Borko (Ed.) **Computer Applications in the Behavioral Sciences.** Englewood Cliffs: Prentice-Hall, 1962, pp. 360-393.

Stone, Philip J.: Dunphy, Dexter C.; Smith, Marshall S.; and Ogilvie, Daniel M. **The General Inquirer: A Computer Approach to Content Analysis.** Cambridge, MA: MIT Press, 1966.

Super, Donald E. *A Theory of Vocational Development.* **American Psychologist,** 1953, 8, 185-190.

Super, Donald E. **The Psychology of Careers.** New York: Harper and Row, 1957.

Super, Donald E.; Crites, John O.; Hummel, Raymond C.; Moser, Helen P.; Overstreet, Phoebe L.; and Warnath, Charles F. **Vocational Development: A Framework for Research.** New York: Teachers College, Columbia University, Bureau of Publications, 1957.

Super, Donald E.; Starishevsky, Reuban; Matlin, Norman; and Jordaan, Jean Pierre. **Career Development: Self Concept Theory.** New York: College Entrance Examination Board, 1963.

Tarule, Jill. *Toward a Philosophy for Testing Programs.* Cambridge, MA: Harvard Graduate School of Education, 1968. (mimeo)

Taylor, E. F. **The ELIZA Program: Conversational Tutorial. IEEE International Convention Record,** 1967, 6 (part 10), 8-15.

Tiedeman, David V. Note in Joint Commision on Mental Illness and Health. **Action for Mental Health.** New York: Basic Books, 1961, p. 126.

Tiedeman, David V. *Predicament Problem, and Psychology: The Case for Paradox in Life and Counseling Psychology.* Journal of **Counseling Psychology**, 1967, 14, 1-8.

Tiedeman, David V. *Career Education: A Guidance Idea Reaches Its Term.* **Quest,** 1974, 7 (3), 1-4.

Tiedeman, David V.; and Dudley, Gordon A. *Thought, Choice, and Action: Processes of Exploration and Commitment in Career Development.* Cambridge, MA: Harvard Graduate School of Education, 1967. (multilith)

Tiedeman, David V.; and Field, Frank L. *From a Technology of Guidance in Schools to the Profession of Guidance-in-Society: A Challenge to Democratic Government.* In McGowan, John F. (project director). **Counselor Development in American Society.** Washington, DC: U.S. Department of Labor, 1965, pp. 249-275.

Tiedeman, David V.; Landy, Edward; Fletcher, Wallace J.; Ellis, Allan B.; Davis, Russell F.; and Boyer, E. Gil (Principal Investigators). **An Information System for Vocational Decisions.** (A Development Program Submitted to the U.S. Commissioner of Education under the Provisions of Section 4 (c) of the Vocational Education Act of 1963). Cambridge, MA: Office for Research Contracts, Harvard University, 1965.

Tiedeman, David V.; and O'Hara, Robert P. **Career Development: Choice and Adjustment.** New York: College Enrance Examination Board, 1963.

Tiedeman, David V.; Schreiber, Marilyn; and Wessell, Tyrus R., Jr. **Key Resources in Career Education: An Annotated Guide.** Washington, DC: National Institute of Education, 1976.

Turing, A. M. *Computing Machinery and Intelligence.* In Anderson, Alan Ross. (Ed.) **Minds and Machines.** Englewood Cliffs, NJ: Prentice-Hall, Inc, 1964, 4-30.

United States Government, Department of Labor, Bureau of Employment Security. **Dictionary of Occupational Titles, I and II** (3rd ed.). Washington, DC: United States Government Printing Office, 1965.

Venn, Grant. **Man, Education, and Manpower.** Washington, DC: American Association of School Administrators, 1970. (ED 044 782.)

Walz, Gary R.; and Rich, Juliet V. *The Impact of Information Systems in Counselor Preparation and Practice.* **Counselor Education and Supervision,** 1967, 6, 275-284.

Weizenbaum, J. *Symmetric List Processor.* **Communications of the ACM,** 1963, 6, 524-544.

Weizenbaum, J. *ELIZA-A Computer Program for the Study of Natural Language.* **Communications of the ACM,** 1966, 9, 36-45.

Weizenbaum, J. *Contextual Understanding by Computer.* **Communications of the ACM,** 1967, 8, 474-480.

White, Robert W. *Ego and Reality in Psychoanalytic Theory: A Proposal Regarding Independent Ego Energies,* **Psychological Issues,** 3, Monograph 11, 1963.

Wrenn, C. Gilbert. **The Counselor in a Changing World.** Washington, DC: American Personnel and Guidance Association, 1962.

INDEX

NOTES

NOTES

NOTES

NOTES